Tours

☀ INSIGHT GUIDES

KRAKOW

StepbyStep

APA PUBLICATIONS L
Part of the Langenscheidt Publishing Group

CONTENTS

ABOUT THIS BOOK

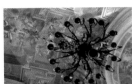

Above: Wawel Hill; ceiling of the Piarists' Church; Dominican Church cloisters; Cloth Hall detail; Tent Room in the Czartoryski Museum.

This *Step by Step Guide* has been produced by the editors of Insight Guides, whose books have set the standard for visual travel guides since 1970. With top-quality photography and authoritative recommendations, this guidebook brings you the very best of Krakow in a series of 16 tailor-made tours.

WALKS AND TOURS

The tours in the book provide something to suit all budgets, tastes and trip lengths. As well as covering Krakow's many classic attractions, the routes track lesser-known sights and up-and-coming areas; there are also excursions for those who want to extend their visit outside the city.

The tours embrace a range of interests, so whether you are an art fan, an architecture buff, a gourmet, a compulsive shopper or have kids to entertain, you will find an option to suit.

We recommend that you read the whole of a tour before setting out. This should help you to familiarise yourself with the route and enable you to plan where to stop for refreshments –

options for this are shown in the 'Food and Drink' boxes, recognisable by the knife-and-fork sign, on most pages.

For our pick of the walks by theme, consult Recommended Tours For… *(see pp.6–7)*.

OVERVIEW

The tours are set in context by this introductory section, giving an overview of the city to set the scene, plus background information on food and drink and shopping. A succinct history timeline in this chapter highlights the key events that have shaped Krakow over the centuries.

DIRECTORY

Also supporting the tours is a Directory chapter, comprising a user-friendly, clearly organised A-Z of practical information, our pick of where to stay while you are in the city and select restaurant listings; these eateries complement the more low-key cafés and restaurants that feature within the tours themselves and are intended to offer a wider choice for evening dining.

The Author

A linguist by training, Craig Turp has spent most of his adult life studying the languages and peoples of Central and Eastern Europe. He has written a number of books on the region and is a key member of the team behind *In Your Pocket*, a series of independent, locally produced city guides. Of Krakow he says: 'Whenever I visit I am reminded of Namatianus writing of Rome: "To count the splendours of this city is to count the stars in the sky."'

He would like to thank the team at *Poland In Your Pocket*, especially Alex Webber and Karolina Montygierd, for their help. Many of the tours in this book were originally conceived by Poland specialist Ian Wisniewski.

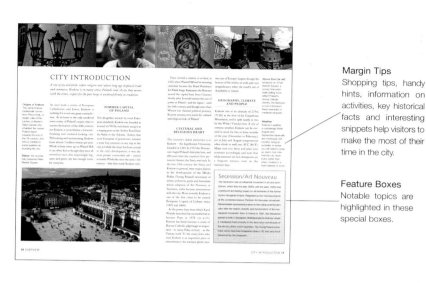

Margin Tips
Shopping tips, handy hints, information on activities, key historical facts and interesting snippets help visitors to make the most of their time in the city.

Feature Boxes
Notable topics are highlighted in these special boxes.

Key Facts Box
This box gives details of the distance covered on the tour, plus an estimate of how long it should take. It also states where the route starts and finishes, and gives key travel information, such as which days are best to do the route or handy transport tips.

Route Map
Detailed cartography shows the tour clearly plotted with numbered dots. For more detailed mapping, see the pull-out map slotted inside the back cover.

Food and Drink
Recommendations of where to stop for refreshment are given in these boxes. The numbers prior to each restaurant/café name link to references in the main text. On city maps, restaurants are plotted.

The € signs at the end of each entry reflect the approximate cost of a two-course meal for two, with a good bottle of wine. These should be seen as a guide only. Price ranges, also quoted on the inside back flap for easy reference, are as follows:

€€€€	over 170zł
€€€	100–170zł
€€	50–100zł
€	50zł

Footers
Those on the left-hand page usually give the tour name, plus, where relevant, a map reference; those on the right-hand page mostly show the main attraction on the double page.

SOMETHING DIFFERENT

Make a beeline for the Socialist Realist enclave of Nowa Huta (walk 13), or Poland's oldest salt mine at Wieliczka (tour 16).

RECOMMENDED TOURS FOR...

THE RICH AND FAMOUS

Take dinner at Wierzynek (walk 1), the city's most expensive and exquisite restaurant, before spending fortunes in the boutiques of ul. Grodzka (walk 7).

COURTING COUPLES

Moonlit walks around the Planty (walk 11) are what romance is all about, while a kiss by Sigismund's Bell (walk 3) is said to guarantee eternal love.

ART LOVERS

Start at the Czartoryski Museum (walk 2), which is one of just five in Europe to possess a Leonardo, before taking in the equally impressive Matejko and Wyspianksi museums (walk 10).

JEWISH KRAKOW

Kazimierz (walk 4) was for centuries Krakow's Jewish heart; the Old Synagogue remains a symbol of the city. Don't forgo the poignant former ghetto area around Rynek Podgórski (walk 12), or Auschwitz (tour 15).

NIGHT OWLS

Main Market Square (tour 1) is surrounded on all sides by cafés and bars that stay open late; Kazimierz (tour 4) is considered the real home of Krakow nightlife by those in the know, however.

GOURMANDS

Main Market Square (walk 1), with its rich variety of restaurants and cafés, is a foodie's dream, while a number of delicatessens on ul. Floriańska (walk 2) stock a wide range of tasty Polish treats to take home.

CATHOLIC VISITORS

Visit John Paul II's student digs (walk 7), the site of his first Mass as a newly qualified priest (walk 3), and go to Mass yourself at St Mary's Church (walk 1).

CHILDREN

The Dragon's Cave (walk 3) up on Wawel Hill is a hit with children of all ages; while both Planty (walk 11) and Jordan Parks (walk 5) have plenty for kids to do.

SHOPPING

The little stores of Wawel Hill (walk 3) and the Cloth Hall in Main Market Square (walk 1) offer fine local wares, while the huge Galeria Krakówska (walk 11) has all your favourite international brands.

OVERVIEW

An overview of Krakow's geography, customs and culture, plus illuminating background information on food and drink, shopping, entertainment and history.

CITY INTRODUCTION

A city of joy and faith, where religion and culture long ago displaced trade and commerce, Krakow is in many senses Poland's soul. A city that moves with the times, respect for the past keeps it anchored firmly in tradition.

Origins of Krakow
The name Krakow traditionally comes from Prince Krak, or Grakh, ruler of the Lechici, a Western Slavic people who inhabited the Lesser Poland region towards the end of the 7th century, and who is credited in some quarters as founding the city.

Below: the wonderfully preserved Main Market Square.

At once both a centre of European Catholicism and Jewry, Krakow is nothing if it is not one giant contradiction. At its heart is the only medieval town centre of Poland's major cities to survive the horrors of the 20th century, yet Krakow is nevertheless a forward-thinking and outward-looking city. Welcoming and mesmerising, Krakow hosts almost 3 million visitors per year. While at busy times up on Wawel Hill it can often feel as though they have all arrived at once, this surprisingly big, open and green city has enough room for everyone.

FORMER CAPITAL OF POLAND

Not altogether ancient by most European standards, Krakow was founded in around AD 950 by merchants using it as a staging post on the Amber Road from the Baltic to the Adriatic. Amber, that most European of gemstones, remains a must-buy souvenir on any trip to the city, yet while the stone has been crucial to the city's development, it was the more prosaic commodity salt – mined at nearby Wieliczka since the early 11th century – that first made Krakow rich.

Fame arrived a century or so later, in 1038, when Wawel Hill and its stunning cathedral became the Royal Residence for Polish kings. Kazimierz the Restorer moved the capital here from Gniezno shortly after. It would remain the seat of power in Poland – and the region – until the 16th century, and though since then Warsaw has claimed political primacy, Krakow remains very much the cultural and religious hub of Poland.

CULTURAL AND RELIGIOUS HEART

The country's oldest university is in Krakow – the Jagellonian University, founded in 1364. In 1533 the Dominicans staged Poland's first play here, and 200 years later the country's first permanent theatre, the Stary, was built. In the late 19th century the Stary, and Krakow in general, were major players in the development of the Młoda Polska (Young Poland) movement of artists, architects, poets and dramatists whose adaption of Art Nouveau, or Secession, styles became synonymous with the city. More recently, Krakow is one of the few cities to be named European Capital of Culture twice (1992 and 2000).

As the power-base from which Karol Wojtyła launched his successful bid to become Pope in 1978 *(see p.13)*, Krakow has lately become a centre of Roman Catholic pilgrimage as important – to many Poles at least – as the Vatican itself. To the many Jews who visit, Krakow is an important place of remembrance: the wartime ghetto here was one of Europe's largest, though the horrors of life within its walls pale into insignificance when the nearby site of Auschwitz is visited.

GEOGRAPHY, CLIMATE AND PEOPLE

Krakow sits at an altitude of 219m (713ft) at the foot of the Carpathian Mountains, and is split neatly in two by the Wisła (Vistula) river. A city of extreme weather, Krakow can be covered in snow for two or three months of the year (December to February), yet in July and August temperatures often climb to well over 30°C (86°F). Make sure you dress and plan your activities accordingly, and note that while summers are hot, downpours are a frequent menace, even on the warmest days.

Above from far left: lamppost on Small Market Square; a young Cracovian; stalls selling icons reflect Poland's strong Catholic identity; the Barbican is one of Europe's finest examples of medieval ramparts.

Weather
Krakow's weather is surprisingly fickle. August and September especially are notoriously wet months: bring an umbrella. In winter you will need to wrap up warm, but note that the city never looks better than when covered in a fresh blanket of snow.

Secession/Art Nouveau

The Secession was an influential movement in art and architecture, which from the late 1890s until the early 1920s had a profound and lasting impact on all territories of the former Austro-Hungarian Empire. Regarded as the Viennese branch of the contemporaneous Parisian Art Nouveau movement, Secessionism represented a return to the notion of art for art's sake after the realism, linearity and functionalism of the neo-classical movement. Born in Vienna in 1897, the Secession spread quickly to Budapest, Bratislava and to Krakow, where it manifested itself primarily in the decorative architecture of the old city centre, and in Kazimierz. The Young Poland movement, led by Stanisław Wyspiański *(see p.73)*, was very much influenced by the Secession.

Local Guides

Those looking for something a bit particular, or off the beaten track, can book a professional local guide. There are hundreds touting their trade, though not all are good. Recommended is Agnieszka Drzaszcz, tel: 060 021 24 98.

Home to 750,000 people, making it the second-largest city in Poland, and the largest in Lesser, or Southern, Poland, Krakow was once one of the most cosmopolitan cities in Poland. Today, however, almost all of Krakow's inhabitants are Poles. Until 1941 and the Holocaust, the Jews were a significant ethnic group: at the beginning of World War II a quarter of the city's population was Jewish. Though some of the hundreds of thousands of Jews who visit each year are now staying on, less than a thousand call the city home permanently.

A CITY OF MANY SIGHTS

For a city born of trade, it is only fitting – today more so than ever – that the centre of Krakow be the sublime Main Market Square (Rynek Główny). Its centrepiece, the astonishingly designed Cloth Hall, is for many as much a symbol of Krakow and its past as Wawel Cathedral. One of 55 buildings graded by Unesco as 'the highest class', it is the first stop for most on explorations of the Old Town, a gorgeous grid of narrow streets all with treasures to hide. Main Market Square is also home to the 13th-century St Mary's, Krakow's main civic church and a fiercely Gothic reminder of the city's past. The prominence given to a statue of national poet Adam Mickiewicz – which stands in the middle of Main Market Square – nods towards Krakow's links with the Polish literary movement, and its status as the nation's cultural capital.

Below: the faces of Krakow.

The Planty

Uniquely among Europe's older quarters, a green belt, the Planty, surrounds the Old Town and provides respite and definition. It was laid out at the beginning of the 19th century to replace the old, and by then redundant, city walls, Krakow having already long ago expanded in all directions. The park is itself surrounded by a ring of major boulevards, beyond which the more modern parts of the city have their own gems to offer, not least to lovers of Secession-era architecture.

Beyond the Old Town

There is much more to Krakow than the Old Town. There is Wawel Hill, home to an imposing castle and cathedral, adorned with some of Europe's finest works of art since Jagiellonian times. At its base is the district of Okół, probably the site of the first settlement in Krakow. There is the old Jewish quarter of Kazimierz, for centuries located outside the city's walls and boasting a distinctive character. Now experiencing a renaissance, it is the city's liveliest district and a popular night-time haunt of students, bohemians and arty types, who throng to its many bars and cafés.

West of Old Town is Piasek, where fine old apartment buildings surround quiet, hidden courtyards that can usually be explored. Nowy Swiat (New Town) was where rich Cracovians moved to in the 19th century when the Old Town became too crowded. Across the river is the site of the Jewish ghetto in Podgórze, made famous by the film *Schindler's List*.

BRIGHT LIGHTS AND LATE NIGHTS

Enormously popular with young visitors, and home for much of the year to a large student population, Krakow over the past decade has become something of a nightlife Mecca. Its clubs and bars buzz with life from dusk to dawn most nights of the week, while fittingly for what is the cultural capital of Poland, Krakow does not lack entertainment choices. Cabaret, theatre, opera and music venues are dotted throughout the city.

Fairs and Festivals

Throughout the year colourful fairs are held on Krakow's streets, none more so than the blessing of palms on Palm Sunday. On Easter Monday, the Emmaus Fair in Zwiernyniec Park brings a colourful end to the Holy Week, while Corpus Christi is marked with a parade from Wawel to Main Market Square. In December, stalls selling local treats and gifts fill the main market square. An organ music festival takes place every March and April.

Dining Out

Krakow has a deserved reputation as a great place to dine out. While Polish cuisine itself is not generally regarded as being particularly good, Krakow has benefited from the influences of the Hapsburg Empire, with Viennese and Hungarian specialities finding their way onto the city's menus, often in the form of tasty local adaptations. Look out for game dishes such as *kaczka* (roast duck).

AROUND KRAKOW

With recently improved transport connections, Krakow is as good a base as any to explore much of southern Poland, and a number of places are accessible on easy day trips: the mountain resort of Zakopane, the former concentration camp at Auschwitz, the Wieliczka Salt Mine and the Socialist-Realist 'new town' of Nowa Huta. Slightly further afield are no fewer than six national parks, the industrial city of Katowice and Krakow's former rival, Tarnów, which has much charm of its own.

Above from far left: the neo-Renaissance façade of the Juliusz Słowacki Theatre; colourful painted Easter eggs; Main Market Square, with the Cloth Hall on the left and St Mary's on the right.

Pope John Paul II

Born Karol Wojtyła in Wadowice, 40km (25 miles) southwest of Krakow, in 1920, Pope John Paul II served as pontiff from 1978 until his death in 2005. Wojtyła moved to Krakow as a student in 1939 to study literature at the Jagellonian University, taking modest accommodation at ul. Tyniecka 10, just across the Vistula from the Grunwaldzki bridge. The house is marked with a plaque. After completing his (clandestine) seminary studies in 1946, he preached his first Mass in the chapel at Wawel Cathedral. Bishop of Krakow from 1958, and cardinal from 1967, he became pope in 1978. His 2002 visit to the city remains a defining moment in its history: his sermon at Błonie meadow was attended by over 2 million. His birthplace and former home have been opened as a museum, featuring childhood photographs and personal effects. Find it on ul. Kościelna 7, Wadowice, an easy day trip from Krakow's main bus station.

FOOD AND DRINK

Polish food, based on simple ingredients and distinct flavours, is both hearty and tasty. In Krakow, local specialities are complemented by a wide range of international restaurants serving fine cuisine.

Above: if you're in need of a quick bite, look out for stalls selling *precels* or *oscypek* (smoked cheese).

Ready and Waiting
Most waiting staff in Krakow speak fairly good English, and usually a smattering of German, too. Menus can usually be found in English (of a sort), and staff never seem to mind helping out if you want to make sure you didn't just order sheep's brain.

You will not go hungry in Krakow. The city's wide range of good restaurants continues to expand, and with a number of the top hotels hiring some of the world's best chefs to oversee their kitchens, you can usually expect top quality, though often at a price. Many of the restaurants of the Old Town are notoriously expensive, though those on tighter budgets will always find *pierogi* – the classic Polish dumpling – in plentiful supply. Krakow is synonymous with coffee culture, and there are small cafés and patisseries all over the city.

Menus are available in English and German in almost all restaurants in the Old Town, and in many more besides. Poles love to dine alfresco, and the city's restaurants and cafés will place tables outside on the street as soon as the weather is warm enough (usually by the end of April, sometimes even earlier).

POLISH SPECIALITIES

Stews, Dumplings and Soups

Pork, potatoes and cabbage are the country's staples, and the national dish is *bigos*, a chunky stew of pork, cabbage, potatoes and onions, spiced with herbs and served with lashings of sour cream. Though it originates in eastern Poland, where winters are long, it is found everywhere. *Pierogi* are similarly ubiquitous, small, semicircular ravioli-like dumplings stuffed with meat, cheese or sometimes fruit. You can pick them up for almost nothing at special *pierogi* bars. Look out, too, for *barscz*, a delicious red beetroot soup flavoured with lemon and garlic and served both hot and cold. Chicken soup is another great Polish favourite.

Game and Sausages

Given that the forests and lakes to the south and east of Krakow are full of game, the local penchant for pheasant, duck (often roasted and served with apples), venison and even boar is understandable. Availability is seasonal, and autumn is the best time to try game dishes, which are usually served with rich sauces and simple vegetables. Polish sausages are excellent, with the heavily smoked *Gruba Krakowska* a local speciality.

Snacks and Sweets

For snacks, look out for *precel* stalls selling delicious hot and vaguely sweet pretzels, usually topped with salt, or *zapiekanki*, a Polish version of pizza. Desserts in Poland tend to be very sweet indeed, such as *kremówka*, cream cakes often covered in syrup or honey.

INTERNATIONAL CUISINE

Krakow is home to some of Poland's best restaurants, boasting a range of cuisines to rival any city in Europe. From cutting-edge Modern European to Pacific Rim Fusion, new flavours are forever being created in the city's best kitchens, which are, as a rule, in the restaurants of the five-star hotels. Catering for the large numbers of Jewish visitors, there is a good range of Jewish restaurants, centred on Kazimierz, although not all are strictly kosher. There are good Indian restaurants, too – an option for vegetarians, who otherwise struggle – as well as some super German-owned beer halls selling sausages with lashings of sauerkraut.

DRINKING

Vodka is the national spirit (Poles claim it was first produced here), but beer is the more popular day-to-day drink, and it's both cheap and – by and large – good. Good popular local brews include Tyskie, Warka and Żywiec, and all have a clear, crisp and refreshing taste. Imported beers, especially Heineken and Stella Artois, are now far more popular with trendy locals, however. Guinness is widely available, not just in Irish pubs (of which there are plenty), but is relatively expensive. Poland produces little wine of its own – none of note – and all wines sold in restaurants and bars are imported. Poles love wine, however, so there is always a good selection on offer; some restaurants have cellars

to die for. Coffee is usually preferred to tea, which is viewed as very much a medicinal drink in these parts.

Café Culture

In Krakow, coffee, and the café, is king. A legacy of the Hapsburg period, locals will visit a café on their way to work, at lunchtime and on their way home. Yet café culture in Krakow is so much more than drinking coffee: the city's cafés are debating chambers, reading rooms and places of inspiration. Some, such as Noworolski *(see p.28)* and Jama Michalika *(see p.68)* are living museums.

(see p.28) ... *(see p.68)*

Above from far left: fried meat stall on Main Market Square; *pierogi*, a Polish speciality; enjoying alfresco drinks on a balmy evening.

Alfresco at a Price
Note that many venues operate a dual pricing policy, with higher prices (or a simple surcharge) being applied to those sitting outside. Check before ordering.

Vodka

Poles like to boast that they invented vodka, at some time in the 14th century, though in truth the various countries of the entire grain-growing region of eastern Poland, southern Lithuania, Belarus and Russia have equally good claims. Made from water, grain, molasses and potatoes or sugar beet, vodka was first used as a medicine, becoming fashionable as a recreational drink only in the 16th century. Famous Polish blends include *Starka* and *Goldwasser*, though the most famous is *Żubrówka*, or Bison Grass Vodka. Mass-produced since 1926 it is the country's best vodka, and though usually drunk neat and chilled, it is sometimes served with apple juice, creating a drink known locally as *Szarlotka*.

ENTERTAINMENT

Krakow is Poland's cultural capital and home to the country's liveliest nightlife. From the cabaret and theatre of the Old Town to Kazimierz's trendy bars and jazz clubs, there is something for everyone.

Hapsburg Legacy
Krakow's lack of a permanent opera house is a legacy of the Hapsburg era, when it was fashionable for wealthy Cracovians to travel to Prague or Vienna to watch opera.

Below: posters for classic plays.

Quite simply, when it comes to things to do when the sun goes down in Krakow, most people find themselves spoilt for choice. From gangs of lads on stag weekends – who don't know which of the city's many strip clubs to go to next – to sophisticated city breakers forced to choose between the philharmonic and the opera, there is plenty of everything for everyone.

THEATRE AND CABARET

The Stary Teatr (ul. Jagiellonska 1; tel: 012 422 85 66) is the oldest theatre in Poland, and home for the country's best stage actors. Though performances are usually in Polish, there are times during the year when local cultural centres sponsor performances in other languages. Even if you are not attending a play, both the Stary, as well as the Słowacki Theatre (pl. Świętego Ducha 1; tel: 021 424 45 00) are worth visiting to admire the sheer sumptuousness of their interiors.

There is a century-long history of cabaret in Krakow that continues to this day, with four cabaret theatre companies putting on regular performances. The best (and most regular) are those at the Piwnica pod Wrywigroszem (św. Jana 30; tel: 012 421 25 00).

MUSIC AND OPERA

The Szymanowski Philharmonic Orchestra plays at the concert hall of the same name (ul. Zwierzyniecka 1; tel: 012 422 09 58), a cavernous venue that suffers from not always being full. There are performances most evenings, with well attended matinée concerts on Sundays. Krakow's opera has no permanent home and usually performs at the Słowacki Theatre. The company's repertoire is limited to the classics, but with ticket prices cheap and standards high it is a good option for a more cerebral evening out.

Jazz

Jazz fans are in for a treat in Krakow, and the Jazz Club u Muniaka (ul. Florianska 3; tel: 012 423 12 05) is one of

the best in Europe, and celebrated Polish and international jazzmen play here every Friday and Saturday night. Look out, too, for Harris Jazz Bar on Main Market Square, a groovy cellar jazz club that seems always to be full.

NIGHTLIFE

Old Town Krakow allegedly has more bars and pubs per square mile than any other city in Europe. We are inclined to believe the legend. You simply cannot swing a cat in this city without hitting a bar, and so seeking out only the best is a wise option. Our favourites are: the Irish-owned Nic Nowego (ul. Kryźa 15; tel: 012 421 61 88) for good drinks, good food and a generally good time; the C.K. Browar beer hall (ul. Podwale 6-7; tel: 012 429 52 05) for a raucous pint with locals and visitors; trendy Paparazzi (ul. Mikołajska 9; tel: 012 429 45 97) for a more sophisticated evening sipping cocktails and champagne; and the legendary Someplace Else at the Sheraton hotel for an expense-account splurge with Krakow's expatriate community which congregates here to watch live sports. You should also head over to Kazimierz for at least a couple of drinks, and try out one or two of the bars on plac Nowy. Great cocktails get served at Le Scandale (pl. Nowy 9; tel: 012 430 68 55), while Zbilizenia (pl. Nowy 7; tel: 012 430 01 38) and Etcetera (pl. Nowy 8; tel: 012 421 32 31) attract trendsetting crowds. Pop into Ginger (pl. Nowy 7), too: one of the smallest bars in the world.

Clubbing

Make sure you put your best dancing shoes on before heading out clubbing (Krakow's doormen are fussy about these things), and make your first stop Prozak (pl. Dominikanski 6; tel: 012 429 11 28), as everybody else does. A little more select are Cien (ul. św. Jana 15; tel: 012 422 21 77), a place the city's beautiful set has made its own, and Fusion Club (ul. Florianska 15; tel: 012 422 44 60), where only the best-dressed and trendiest are selected for entry.

CINEMA

In the centre of Krakow the fine old Sztuka movie hall (ul. św Jana 6; tel: 012 421 41 99; www.ars.pl) dates from 1916 and shows Hollywoood blockbusters as well as art-house movies. Multi-screen cinemas include the enormous Cinema City at the Krakow Plaza (ul. Pokuju 44; tel: 012 290 90 90; www.cinema-city.pl) shopping centre east of the city. Films are usually shown in their original language with Polish subtitles.

Above from far left: the city brims with bars and jazz clubs.

Nightlife Listings Krakow's nightlife scene is subject to incessant changes, so make sure you pick up a copy of *Krakow In Your Pocket* when in town for the latest on where's hot, and where's not.

Football

Krakow, like most of Poland, is football (soccer) crazy, with the local team Wisla Krakow regularly challenging for (and in recent years usually winning) the Polish league title. Patronised by a wealthy local businessman who has invested heavily in the club, Wisla plays at the city's main stadium in Jordan Park, and though games are well attended they are not usually sell-outs, so getting a ticket should be easy; they cost very little. The season runs from July to May, with a break in December and January.

SHOPPING

While never hoping to rival London, Paris (or even Warsaw) as a shopping destination, there is plenty to spend your money on in Krakow; it has modern shopping centres as well as small boutiques and specialist stores.

Buy Local
Imported goods can often be as expensive as they are in their country of origin, so you shouldn't expect to buy international brand names at a knock-down rate in Krakow. Polish-produced goods are often considerably cheaper, and an increasing range of the country's brand names offer quality as well as classic or innovative design.

Christmas Shop
Galeria Calik, at 5 Main Market Square, sells handcrafted Christmas decorations. Baubles and trinkets made of gold and decorated with amber and other precious stones can be made to order. Many of the world's richest people order their decorations from the store.

Nobody comes to Krakow to shop, or at least they didn't: word in hip quarters of New York, London and Paris right now is that Kazimierz is an increasingly fine place to pick up a wide selection of Hapsburg-era antiques. Beyond antiquities and ubiquitous amber – the national gemstone – you should look out for leather goods and accessories, tableware, glassware and lace.

CLOTH HALL AND THE MARKETS

First stop for many visitors – shopping or not – Cloth Hall offers a fair selection of tourist tat on its ground floor, most of which is now adorned with the face of Pope John Paul II, with most of the good stuff hidden upstairs, reserved for the more enquiring traveller. Look out for good-quality folk art, carved wooden sculptures and tasteful religious art. Krakow's other markets tend to sell produce only, but are great if you want to see real people actually living daily lives in this most touristy of cities. The largest is that on ul. Gregorczkecka, a short walk east of the city centre. Flea and occasional markets are a regular sight in Main Market Square, and note that throughout December in the run-up

to Christmas the square fills up with small stallholders selling local delicacies and other handmade gifts.

SHOPPING STREETS

The principal shopping thoroughfares in the city centre are ul. Floriańska, Main Market Square and ul. Grodzka, which link up conveniently to form a 'shopping triangle'. It's worth shopping at any number of the stores in these streets, but it can be difficult to recommend specific outlets and locations, for two reasons: it's not uncommon for shops here to have no street number, which can be confusing; some stores, in keeping with the legacy of the Communist era, display only generic titles such as 'Jeweller', and don't seem to have a proprietary name.

There are two big, modern shopping centres within easy access of the Old Town: Galeria Krakowska, opposite the main railway station *(see p.79)*, and Galeria Kazimierz, which offers a free bus shuttle service from Plac Matejki.

Opening Hours
Typical opening hours are Mon–Fri 10am–7pm, Sat 10am–6pm. Small shops are closed on Sunday, but the big shopping centres are open until late. Most shops now accept credit cards.

WHAT TO BUY

Leather and Fur

Elegant leather goods including hand-bags, gloves, coats, jackets and luggage are all worth taking a look at, while fur and winter hats, sheepskin coats, jackets and accessories are slightly cheaper than elsewhere. In Poland wearing fur is not seen as a sin: almost every woman – of every age – owns a fur hat and coat.

Jewellery

Items made from amber *(see box below)* often represent exceptionally good value, whether it is in the form of rings, earrings, necklaces, bracelets, cuff-links, or even lampshades and jewellery boxes. You will have no trouble finding amber in Krakow: the best is in the small shops of the Old Town, such as Amber Inspi-rations, in Cloth Hall on Main Market Square, and at ul. Floriańska 42.

Antiques

A wide range of small shops in the city centre house all sorts of wonderful knick-knacks, from Soviet- and even Nazi-era memorabilia to antique watches and clocks. While, technically, you cannot export items produced before 1945 – unless you gain written permission from the appropriate government department beforehand – small personal items such as medals, badges, watches and pens are usually exempt. Any reputable antique shop will be able to arrange authorisation and onward shipping, although usually at some cost.

Sweets and Vodka

Confectionery made at the famous Krakow Wawel sweet factory is a good buy, as is the generally excellent Polish vodka. Note that with vodka price is directly related to quality *(see also p.15)*.

Above from far left: the Cloth Hall has been a centre of commerce since medieval times; traditional lace-making; an open-air art stall; ul. Grodzka is a good place to head for boutiques.

Flower Women
The tradition of selling flowers between the Cloth Hall and St Mary's Church on Krakow's Main Market Square is believed to have started back in the first half of the 16th century. It is the sole preserve of women known as Krakowskie Kwia-ciarki, or the Krakow Flower Women (*kwiat* means 'flower').

Baltic Gold

Amber, Poland's national gemstone, is fossilised resin that once seeped from de-ciduous and coniferous trees, solidified and, over the course of thousands of years, matured into the form we are familiar with today. This resin sometimes traps insects and flora, and amber that contains identifiable specimens of prehistoric life is con-

sidered a special rarity, and priced accordingly. The sea washes up amber from beneath the surface of the sand, depositing it conveniently on beaches to be collected. The colour of the luminous, transparent stone ranges across a surprising spectrum, from yellow and white to stones with red and green streaks and tinges. These tints aren't flaws; they add char-acter to the stone.

HISTORY: KEY DATES

With a rich but much troubled history, Krakow still bears some of the scars from battles fought over its cultural and religious landmarks. Most have fortunately, miraculously even, survived.

EARLY KRAKOW

50,000 BC	First known settlement on Wawel Hill, Palaeolithic era.
9th century AD	Wawel Hill becomes a fortified village and the seat of the Wiślan (Vistulan) Dukes.
965	The earliest written reference to Krakow, by Cordoba merchant Ibrahim ibn Jakub, who describes it as 'a major town known throughout Europe'.
1000	The bishopric of Krakow is founded following Poland's conversion to Christianity in 966.

Below: the Collegium Maius was Poland's first university; a detail from Veit Stoss' triptych altarpiece in St Mary's Church; the Barbican.

MEDIEVAL KRAKOW

Early 11th century	Construction of first cathedral on Wawel Hill.
1038	King Kazimierz Odnowiciel (Casimir the Restorer) moves the capital of Poland from Gniezno to Krakow and builds a royal residence on Wawel Hill.
1086	St Andrew's, one of Poland's earliest Romanesque churches, is founded.
12th century	Wieliczka salt mine is established outside Krakow.
1241	Tartars destroy the town.
1257	Krakow gains municipal rights.
1290	Construction of St Mary's Church begins.
1335	Kazimierz is founded as a separate town outside Krakow.
1386	Inauguration of the Polish-Lithuanian Commonwealth, with Krakow as the capital.
1400	Collegium Maius is established as the second university college in Central and Eastern Europe.
1430	Krakow joins Hanseatic League.

RENAISSANCE AND BAROQUE KRAKOW

1477–89	Gothic triptych altarpiece in St Mary's Church is completed.
1499	The Barbican is completed.

1556–60	The Cloth Hall, designed by Giovanni Maria of Padua (Padovano), is built in Renaissance style.
1596	King Zygmunt III Waza transfers the royal residence to Warsaw, which he declares the capital of Poland.
1665–7	Swedish invaders ravage and loot the town.
1734	King August III Saski becomes the last Polish monarch to be crowned in Wawel Cathedral.
1783	Krakow's Botanical Garden is established.

HAPSBURG KRAKOW

1795	After three successive partitions of Poland, Krakow becomes part of the Austro-Hungarian Empire.
1799	Poland's longest-serving theatre, Stary Teatr, is established.
1800	Kazimierz becomes part of Krakow.
1820s	Planty gardens are laid out.
1846	Krakow leads an uprising against the Austro-Hungarian Empire.
1850	The Great Fire devastates the town's historic centre.
1879	Poland's first national museum is established in the Cloth Hall.
1896	Juliusz Słowacki Theatre opens and screens first film in Poland.

20TH-CENTURY KRAKOW

1918	Krakow becomes part of a newly independent Poland.
1939	Nazis establish administrative headquarters in the city.
1945	Red Army liberates Krakow. Rigged election leads to Communist, Soviet-satellite government.
1947–9	The Lenin Steelworks (now known as Sendzimir) are built in the Krakow suburb of Nowa Huta.
1978	Krakow's historic centre gains Unesco World Heritage Status; Cardinal Karol Wojtyła, Bishop of Krakow, is elected pope.
1980	Government recognises Solidarity as a legitimate free trade union.
1981–3	Martial law.
1989	Democratic elections see Solidarity emerge victorious.
1992 & 2000	Krakow is declared a European City of Culture.

Below: a memorial in the district of Kazimierz, which was cleared of its Jewish residents by the Nazis in 1941.

MODERN KRAKOW

2004	Poland joins the EU.
2005	The city's people fill the streets to mourn the death of the pope.
2007	The 750th anniversary of Krakow as a city.

A FABRYKA WYROBÓW C
KAROLA RZA

...la przybory skórzane...

.JHNATOV

WALKS AND TOURS

MAIN MARKET SQUARE

Playing heart to Wawel's soul, Main Market Square has been Krakow's commercial and social centre for centuries. Every building has a story and in many cases great historical importance; all visits to Krakow should start here.

DISTANCE 1km (½ mile)

TIME A half day

START No.4, by St Mary's

END St Barbara's Church

POINTS TO NOTE

Main Market Square is numbered clockwise from St Mary's Cathedral (no. 4; Cloth Hall takes 1–3). Try to begin this route as early as possible, although note that during summer months even a 7am start will not spare you the crowds. After completing the walk at St Mary's it can be extended by following walk 2. To get an idea of the city's layout and for great panoramic views, climb to the top of the Town Hall Tower.

Cloth Hall Saved

In the period immediately after World War II, plans were drawn up by Poland's newly installed Communist authorities to give the square a more proletarian look by ripping down Cloth Hall and replacing it with a Modernist Town Hall. Fortunately, good sense prevailed and the Cloth Hall survived.

Laid out in 1257 and measuring nearly 40,000sq m (10 acres), **Main Market Square** (Rynek Główny) is one of Europe's largest medieval squares. It is certainly the most impressive. This was once the scene of majestic royal parades, and official guests are still ceremoniously greeted here. On a more everyday level, the square has long been a thriving centre of commercial activity, and continues to bustle with locals as well as tourists.

In summer the buzz goes on late into the night. An abundance of cafés, restaurants, shops, flower stalls and street performers form a colourful, engaging atmosphere, with buskers often appearing as duets and trios and playing exquisite classical refrains.

BURGHERS' HOUSES AND PALACES

The imposing burghers' houses and the grand palaces surrounding the Main Market Square were once owned by the city's wealthiest merchants and aristocratic families, and a variety of façades reflect diverse architectural genres.

Beginning your walk at no. 4 (the first house on the square after St Mary's), the Secession is evident in the fancy design of the upper levels

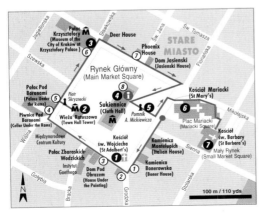

(though the house is in fact pre-Secession, it was redesigned at the beginning of the 20th century).

Crossing ul. Sienna, on the left is where Poland's first post office operated during the 16th and 17th centuries, the **Montelupi** or **Italian House** (Kamienica Montelupich) at no. 7. Postal coaches would enter the rear courtyard through the narrow arch which looks barely big enough for purpose. At no. 9, **Boner House** (Kamienica Bonerowska) has retained the original ornamental attic built in the 1560s, when the house belonged to the king's private banker, Jan Boner. **Bar 13**, see ⑪①, on the corner of the square is a great coffee and cake location for a little early-morning pick me up before moving on.

ST ADALBERT'S

In the far southeastern corner of the square, and looking as though it is sinking into it, little **St Adalbert's Church ❶** (Kościół św Wojciecha; tel: 012 422 83 52; Mon–Sat 7.30am–5pm, Sun 10am–5pm) dates back to the early 12th century. This tiny Romanesque church, resembling an elegant white cube with a Gothic cupola, is a small affair with room for only a few pews. Nevertheless, impressive interiors feature frescoes combining restraint and fully fledged ornamentation.

One such picture depicts St Adalbert being killed by the Prussians after he had baptised them in AD 997. It is believed that an earlier church on this site was the site of St Adalbert's last sermon before he set off with his missionaries to convert the Prussians. The poignant altar features gilded angels standing on either side of a painting of the Madonna and Child.

The Vaults

The vaults of St Adalbert's house an **exhibition** (Mon–Sat 9am–5pm, Sun 1.30–5pm; charge) of the History of Krakow's Market Square, with Romanesque and pre-Romanesque fragments of an even larger stone church, remnants of a wooden church believed to be the first in Krakow, and the wooden remains of an even earlier pagan temple.

THE SOUTHERN FAÇADE

The city's most historic restaurant, **Wierzynek**, behind St Adalbert's and to the right at no. 15, comprises two Renaissance houses. One of the dining rooms features original 14th-century Gothic arches, and the wine bar and grill is situated in a 14th-century cellar,

Above from far left: alfresco cafés line the Main Market Square; performers in traditional dress; flowers for sale; the cupola of St Adalbert's.

Below: details from the façades of burghers' houses and palaces on the square.

Food and Drink 🍴

① BAR 13
Rynek Główny 13; tel: 012 617 02 12; Mon–Sat 9am–9pm, Sun 11am–5pm; €€€€
This is one of the more upmarket cafés on the square, yet remains a good place to unwind while sightseeing around the Old Town. Coffee, tea, cocktails, cakes, sandwiches and huge salads all served at relatively expensive prices.

Above from left:
Town Hall Tower; one of the tower's clocks; post-1945 art in the Museum of the City of Krakow.

Head Inside
Beside the Town Hall Tower is an odd-looking sculpture of a head on its side that on closer inspection can be entered and explored; this is *Eros Bendato* by Igor Mitoraj (1944–), who studied at Krakow's Academy of Art.

Right: House Under the Painting.

see ⑪②. The 16th-century **House Under the Painting** (Dom Pod Obrazem) at no. 19 features a beautiful fresco of the Blessed Virgin Mary ascending into Heaven, held aloft by angels, that was completed in 1718. **Wentzl** on the ground floor sells Krakow's best ice cream, see ⑪③. The **Zbaraski-Wodzicki Palace** at no. 20, which houses the Goethe Institute, was built in the 14th century, though its neoclassical façade dates from the 18th century, when the arcaded court-yard was added.

Following the square around to the western facade, the 14th century **Palace Under the Rams** (Pałac Pod Baranami) at no. 27 was refashioned in the mid-19th century. The court-yard garden is now a café, see ⑪④, and the Cellar Under the Rams (Piwnica Pod Baranami) a cabaret and music venue. Its founder Piotr Skryznecki is honoured with a statue in front of the **Vis-à-Vis** bar next door, see ⑪⑤.

TOWN HALL TOWER

Opposite Vis-à-Vis is all that remains of the magnificent **Town Hall ❷** (Ratusz): the **Town Hall Tower** (Wieża Ratuszowa; tel: 012 619 23 00; May–Oct daily 10.30am–6pm; charge). This handsome red-brick tower is inlaid with decorative stone and is principally 14th-century Gothic, with 16th-century Renais-sance additions. The main town hall was demolished in 1820, at the same time as much of the city's defensive walls and towers, and it was only due to sustained protests by prominent locals that the tower was saved. It doesn't take long to view the tower (and much of that time is spent nego-tiating steep, narrow stairs).

Exhibitions
The first floor, originally a chapel, houses a collection of architectural fragments, though it is now mainly used for exhibitions. The second floor is currently closed to the public. The third floor's photographic exhibition shows how the tower looked during the 19th century, and the top floor offers excellent views of Krakow. Vis-itors can also admire the old clock mechanism, which is radio-controlled from the Mainflingen and synchro-nised with the atomic clock.

MUSEUM OF THE CITY OF KRAKOW

As you walk towards the northern side of the square on leaving the tower, the

last building on the left is the **Krzyszto-fory Palace ❸** (Pałac Krzysztofory), which dates from the 17th century and today houses the **Museum of the City of Krakow at Krzysztofory Palace** (Rynek Główny 35; tel: 012 619 23 00; www.mhk.pl; Sun–Thur 9am–6pm, Fri–Sat 9am–7pm; charge). The upstairs features a permanent exhibition tracing the history of the city from the year it received its royal charter in 1257 until the German invasion of 1939. Among the many exhibits are some fine pieces of furniture and a collection of oil portraits of some of the city's more famous historical characters inside the opulent Fontana Room.

Next door at no. 34 is **Hawełka**, one of the city's most enduring restaurants and great for lunch or dinner, see ⑪⑥.

THE NORTHERN FAÇADE

Though the northern façade is less immediately impressive than the square's other facades, the Baroque **Deer House** at no. 36, once an inn, and the classic town houses at nos 38 and 39 are worthy of inspection, while **Phoenix House** at no. 41 is home to the excellent **Loża Klub Aktora** café, see ⑪⑦.

Next door, the castle-like **Jasienski House** (Dom Jasienski) was another possession of the wealthy Boner family, before later serving as the home and gallery of Feliks Jasienski, a 19th-century art collector. Today fittingly a bank, **No. 47 Rynek Główny**, which sports a wonderful, oversized entrance, was once a mint.

Food and Drink

② WIERZYNEK
Rynek Główny 15; tel: 012 424 96 00; daily 1pm–midnight; €€€€
Older than – we believe – any other restaurant in the city, this place has been serving quality Polish dishes for more than 150 years. It occupies two Renaissance houses, and there is a selection of elegant dining rooms to choose from. For a less formal meal try the grill room in the basement.

③ SŁODKI WENTZL
Rynek Główny 19; tel: 012 429 57 12; daily 10am–11pm; €€€€
Locals insist that this place serves the best ice cream in the city. Try for yourself and see. There is also an upmarket restaurant here (though others around the square are better), and the floors above are occupied by the historic Wentzl hotel (see p.113).

④ PAŁAC POD BARANAMI
Rynek Główny 27 (Courtyard); tel: 069 392 20 10; Sun–Thur 5pm–2am, Fri–Sat 5pm–4am; €€
Actually now called Boro, this is an Old Town legend of a café, bar and club. It is one of the few places in Old Town just as popular with locals as visitors, and has a grit and authenticity that trendier newcomers lack.

⑤ VIS-À-VIS
Rynek Główny 29; tel: 012 422 69 61; daily 8am–11pm; €€
Another Main Market Square café that is just as popular with locals as visitors, and as such is a great place to watch real Cracovians living real lives and generally have a good time.

⑥ HAWEŁKA
Rynek Główny 34 (ground floor); tel: 012 422 06 31; daily 11am–11pm; €€€
Still the first choice for those looking for a formal dining venue, this place long ago lost its crown as the city's best eatery. That said, the food remains very good – if a tad expensive – and the service as stuffy and fussy as you would expect. For a splurge it takes some beating.

⑦ LOZA KLUB AKTORA
Rynek Główny 41; tel: 012 429 29 62; daily 9am–midnight; €€€
One of the newer breed of Krakow cafés, yet one which – with quirks such as the waitresses' cute uniforms – manages to fit in seamlessly with its surroundings. A good range of sandwiches and cakes make it a good lunchtime spot, while later in the day it becomes a trendy drinking venue.

Located in the eastern side of the Cloth Hall is the Małopolska ('Little Poland') Regional Tourist Information Centre (tel: 012 421 77 06; Mon–Fri 9am–6pm, Sat and Sun, 9am–2pm), useful for help on getting round Krakow but also for trips into the region.

Below: coffee and cream cake.

CLOTH HALL

At the centre of Main Market Square is the magnificent **Cloth Hall ❹** (Sukiennice; daily Apr–Oct 10am–7pm, Nov–Mar 11am–6pm). Originally a covered market with stalls, shops and warehouses selling cloth and textiles, this building was first constructed in the mid-13th century. After the hall was almost destroyed by fire, Giovanni Maria of Padua (known as Padovano) designed the current Renaissance façade, including the loggias at either end, in 1556–60. The ornamental attic, decorated with mascarons for which Krakow's most distinguished burghers apparently posed, was the work of Santi Gucci of Florence. The roof also features various copper globes surmounting small spires. During recent renovations it was discovered that these globes contained historical documents from the late 18th to the mid-19th century – there is a long tradition of builders secreting items for posterity in such 'time capsules'.

Ground Floor

The ground floor of the Sukiennice retains its commercial role. Stalls here sell folk arts and crafts, amber and

silver jewellery, leather goods and superior-quality souvenirs. The arcades added in 1875–9 on either side of the building now house attractive cafés. A delightful example, at no. 1, is the Seccessionist-style **Kawiarnia Noworolski**, see ⑪⑧.

First Floor Gallery

The first floor of the Sukiennice is usually home to the **Gallery of 19th-Century Polish Painting and Sculpture** (Galeria Sztuki Polskiej XIX Wieku) but it is currently closed for renovation, scheduled to be completed by the summer of 2009. Poland's first national museum, it opened in 1879, and Jan Matejko, the finest painter in the country's history, was among the artists who donated their own work. The collection, which, in addition to the works of Polish artists such as Matejko, Adam Chmielowski, J. Tatarkiewicz and P. Weloński, features foreign artists in Poland, including the Italian Marcello Bacciarelli, has been moved to the 16th-century royal palace at Niepołomice, 24km (15 miles) southeast of Krakow. Minibuses depart for the palace every 30 minutes throughout the day from Krakow train station.

ADAM MICKIEWICZ MONUMENT

Directly outside the Sukiennice is **Adam Mickiewicz Monument ❺** (Pomnik Adama Mickiewicza), a popular meeting point for locals in the Main Market Square. It honours

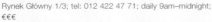

Food and Drink

⑧ **KAWIARNIA NOWOROLSKI**

Rynek Główny 1/3; tel: 012 422 47 71; daily 9am–midnight; €€€

Lenin allegedly drank coffee here, as did untold other revolutionaries and literary types who have so often made Krakow their home. Today it remains much as it has for centuries, and is very much the quintessential Krakow café.

Poland's greatest romantic poet, Adam Mickiewicz *(see box on p.31)*. Designed by Teodor Rygier, it was unveiled in 1898 on the centenary of the poet's birth. The monument is the venue for Krakow's popular pre-Christmas crib competition *(see note on p.31)*.

Other traditional events held in Main Market Square include the colourful Lajkonik pageant shortly after Corpus Christi. This sees a procession of 'Tartars' marching through the streets led by the *lajkonik* – according to legend, one of the Vistula river rafters disguised as a Tartar riding a hobby-horse that dances to the beat of accompanying drums. It's considered good luck to be touched by the *lajkonik*'s wooden mace.

ST MARY'S

In contrast with the diminutive St Adalbert's is the imposing, twin-towered **St Mary's Church** ❻ (Kościół Mariacki; Mon–Sat 11.30am–6pm, Sun 2–6pm; ceremonial opening of the high altar, daily except Sun 11.50am). This church has two entrances, one for tourists at the rear (charge), the other (the main entrance) for regular worshippers or those (excluding tourists) attending Mass. Construction of this triple-naved Gothic basilica began in 1288, incorporating some fragments of an earlier Romanesque church that was burnt during the Tartar invasion of 1221.

St Mary's was privately funded and, according to the medieval Polish chronicler Jan Długosz, it immediately

became the city's principal parish church. The side chapels and towers were only completed in the early 14th century. The shorter of the two is the bell tower; the other, more ornamental tower bears a late-Baroque 'crown' on the spire dedicated to the Virgin Mary, and served as a city watchtower.

Intricate Interiors

The beautiful, intricate interiors demand a leisurely visit for a full appreciation of the various architectural genres, including Gothic, Renaissance and Baroque. The late 19th-century polychromy was designed by the finest Polish artists, including Matejko and Stanisław Wyspiański, with stained-glass windows also designed by Wyspiański and Józef Mehoffer.

Above from far left:
Cloth Hall loggia;
stained-glass
windows in St Mary's.

Mickiewicz Statue
Adam Mickiewicz, whose statue is one of the square's best features, never actually visited Krakow. At least, not during his lifetime: on the 35th anniversary of his death his body was brought here and placed in Wawel Cathedral crypt.

Below: the twin towers of St Mary's.

Veit Stoss's Masterpiece

The church's most extraordinary work of art is the late Gothic triptych altarpiece entitled *The Lives of Our Lady and Her Son Jesus Christ*. This was completed between 1477 and 1489 by the Nuremberg master carver Veit Stoss (known in Poland as Wit Stwosz), who was considered the finest craftsman of his age. The altarpiece incorporates over 200 carved figures (many of them based on contemporary Cracovians) and decorative elements made from linden wood. The central panel, 13m (42ft) high and 11m (36ft) wide, and opened every day at noon depicts the Virgin Mary falling into an eternal sleep, surrounded by the Apostles. It is considered perhaps the finest piece of sculpture ever executed in Poland. Side panels depict scenes from the life of the Virgin Mary and Jesus, including the Annunciation, Nativity, the Adoration of the Magi, Resurrection, and Coronation of the Virgin Mary as Queen of Heaven. Incredibly, a shift in artistic trends during the 17th century saw an attempt to replace the masterpiece with a plasterwork sculpture: only the Swedish invasion of 1655 prevented its total destruction, though part – it was originally much larger – was lost for ever.

Another Stoss masterpiece, a stone cross known as the *Slacker Crucifix* and depicting Christ in some discomfort on the cross, can be seen in the south aisle. After completing the cross and altarpiece, Stoss remained in Krakow, where he worked for the king and aristocrats for a further 20 years.

The Tower and the Trumpeter

Every hour, on the hour, day and night, a trumpeter from the local fire brigade plays the *hejnał*, a short tune, from the taller **tower**. This tradition originates from the time a watchman, seeing the Tartars prepare to scale the city walls at dawn, blew his trumpet to raise the alarm. The Tartars fired a salvo of arrows at the watchman and, after a few notes, he was hit in the throat. Although the tune was cut off in mid-melody, the town was roused from sleep and defended itself. In memory of this event, the *hejnał* is played four times on every hour (to the four sides of the world) and every time it is stopped abruptly.

ST BARBARA'S

Behind St Mary's Church on **Mariacki Square** (Plac Mariacki), laid out at the beginning of the 18th century on the site of the former parish cemetery, is **St Barbara's Church ⑦** (Kościół św Barbary). Apparently the church was constructed with the materials left from the construction of St Mary's Church, and by the same craftsmen. It originated in 1338 as the cemetery chapel, and sermons were given in Polish, in contrast with St Mary's Church, whose German-language sermons reflected the German dominance of the town council. King Zygmunt Stary (Sigismund the Old) reversed this in 1537. St Barbara's was administered by the Jesuits from 1583 until 1773 when the Order was dissolved in Poland. (It returned in 1874.)

Fowl Fortune
The thousands of pigeons which flock to Main Market Square are said to be the courtiers of Henryk Probus, a 13th-century duke who made a pact with a witch in order to raise funds for a trip to the Vatican. When he blew his money on high living and failed to repay his debt to the witch, she turned his courtiers into pigeons.

The small façade features a Renaissance portal as well as 15th-century late Gothic sculptures depicting Christ in the Garden of Gethsemane.

Sacral Art

The Baroque interiors, effectively painted in two shades of blue, also include three Gothic works of sacral art – the *pietà* sculpture, a crucifix, and polychromy depicting the Apprehending of Christ. Additional polychromy on the vaulted ceiling was completed by Piotr Franciszek Molitor

in 1765. The 17th-century main altar has paintings of the Virgin Mary and St Barbara (who died in 1621 and is buried in the crypt), as well as an exquisitely carved altar rail.

Chapel

The 17th-century Chapel of the Blessed Virgin Mary features the miraculous icon of Matka Boska Jurowicka (the Madonna of Jurowice), brought to Krakow in 1885 from the town of Jurowice, where the cult of the Blessed Virgin Mary developed.

Above from far left: the trumpeter plays the *hejnał* from St Mary's taller tower; flowers and jewellery for sale in the square.

Adam Mickiewicz

Few poets have the honour of being declared a nation's eternal poet; Adam Mickiewicz (1798–1855) is probably unique in having the honour bestowed on him in two countries. For just as Mickiewicz is adored in his adopted Poland, so he is revered in Lithuania, the country of his birth, and where he is known as Adomas Mickevičius. His nationality is therefore a moot point, and in these parts a touchy subject. While he is undisputedly a Polish poet (he wrote exclusively in Polish), his ethnicity is in fact unknown, and both Poles and Lithuanians claim him as their own. In fact, evidence suggests that he might well have been of either Belarussian or even Tartar stock. The fact that his most famous poem – *Pan Tadeusz*, written of course in Polish – begins with the line 'O Lithuania, My Fatherland…' only confuses things further.

Christmas Cribs
On the first Thursday of December a highly competitive Christmas crib *(szopka)* competition is held in Main Market Square. Exquisitely decorated *szopki* are brought to the square by amateur craftsmen from all over Lesser Poland. The winning cribs are displayed in the Museum of the City of Krakow *(see p.27).*

SKIRTING THE ROYAL ROUTE

When kingly processions would close the Royal Route, Cracovians would be forced to make lengthy detours. Starting at Small Market Square this walk, packed with little gems, follows one such detour back to Main Market Square.

> **DISTANCE** 1km (½ mile)
> **TIME** A half day
> **START** Small Market Square
> **END** Main Market Square
> **POINTS TO NOTE**
>
> Small Market Square is directly behind St Barbara's Church, which can be seen from Main Market Square. Note that the Czartoryski Museum is not open on Mondays.

This route allows you to view some of the best art and religious architecture in town following a route that – by and large – avoids the crowds that wander without a thought along ul. Floriańska.

SMALL MARKET SQUARE

The start of our walk, the **Small Market Square ❶** (Mały Rynek), served as the city's meat market until the 19th century. Today it hosts some good cafés for a pre-walk primer, including **Albo Tak Café** at no. 4, see ⑭①.

Take a left turn at the square's northern end, on to Mikolajska, and you will be faced by the **Kamienica Hipolitów** (Plac Mariacki 3; tel: 012 422 42 19; Tue–Wed, Fri–Sun 9am–6pm, Thur noon–7pm, closed 2nd Sun of the month; charge), a 17th-century building inside which are re-creations of wealthy burghers' houses from the 16th to the early 20th centuries. Much of the fine furniture on display is original.

CHURCH OF ST THOMAS AND HOLY CROSS CHURCH

Exiting the Kamienica Hipolitów and taking a left, head 100 metres/yds north along ul. Szpitalna, where you'll come

Map labels:

Kościół Pijarów (Piarist's) ❻
Brama Floriańska (Florian's Gate)
Mury Obronne (City Walls) ❺
Basztowa
Szpitalna
Pijarska
Szewska
Muzeum Czartoryskich ❼ ③
Św. Jana
Pałac Lubomirskich ②
Pałac Popielów
Pałac Wodzickich
Św. Marka
Sławkowska
Floriańska
Pomnik A. Fredry
Teatr im. J. Słowackiego (Juliusz Słowacki Theatre) ④
Kościół św. Jana Chrzciciela i św. Jana Ewangelisty (St John the Baptist and St John the Evangelist) ❽
Pl. Św. Ducha
Dom Pod Krzyżem (Museum of Kraków's Theatre)
Kościół św. Krzyża (Holy Cross) ③
Św. Marka
Kościół św. Tomasza Apostoła (St Thomas')
Szpitalna
Św. Krzyża
Św. Tomasza
Floriańska
Rynek Główny (Main Market Square)
Kamienica Hipolitów
Mikołajska
Kościół Mariacki (St Mary's)
Plac Mariacki (Mariacki Square) ①
Sienna
Kościół św. Barbary (St Barbara's) ❶
Mały Rynek (Small Market Square) ❶
Mikołajska
N
100 m / 110 yds

across the **Church of St Thomas the Apostle ②** (Kościół św Tomasza Apostoła) at no. 12. This is a prime example of 17th-century Baroque architecture. A short walk further north is Elektor *(see p.112)*, one of the city's finest hotels.

Continuing along ul. Szpitalna, you'll reach Plac św Ducha (The Holy Spirit's Square). On the right-hand corner of the square is the Dom Pod Krzyżem, today a specialist museum of Cracovian theatre, while the square's real masterpiece is the Gothic **Holy Cross Church ③** (Kościół św Kryża; ul. św Kryża 23) at the rear. Established by the Order of the Canons Regular of the Holy Spirit de Saxia, who arrived in Poland in 1222, the church's inner portal, the chapel of St Mary Magdalene and the baptismal font depicting scenes of the Annunciation, Crucifixion and various saints, are each wonderful examples of Gothic design. Moreover, a chapel dedicated to the founder of the church, St Dominic, is one of the best examples of Polish Renaissance art. The impressive vaulted ceiling, supported by a single pillar, includes 16th-century polychromy alongside 19th-century examples by Stanisław Wyspiański.

JULIUSZ SŁOWACKI THEATRE

Opposite the Holy Cross Church is the **Juliusz Słowacki Theatre ④** (Teatr im J. Słowackiego; Plac św Ducha 1). One of the city's leading theatrical venues, this fabulously eclectic, neo-Renaissance confection

was designed by Jan Zawiejski, who modelled it on the Paris Opera House.

Built in 1893 on the site of a hospital originally run by the Order of the Canons Regular of the Holy Spirit de Saxia, it features crimson and highly gilded interiors, including impressive stage curtains painted with allegories of comedy and tragedy. The theatre screened the first film shown in Poland in 1896, and staged the premiere of Wyspiański's *Wesele (The Wedding)* in 1901. The flower beds at the front of the theatre set off a bust of Aleksander Fredro, a hero of Polish comedy.

FLORIAN'S GATE

Leave the square and continue north along ul. Szpitalna. Turn left into ul. Pijarska and you'll come to **Florian's Gate ⑤** (Brama Floriańska). Having served as the principal entrance to the northern side of the city, this is the only remaining gateway of the town's medieval defensive system, which comprised eight gateways and almost 40 bastions. The gate's northern aspect

Above from far left: Small Market Square; inside the Kamienica Hipolitów; a single pillar supports the vaulted ceiling of the Holy Cross Church; Florian's Gate.

The Actors' Church
The Holy Cross Church is also known as the Actors' Church, and you can see an epitaph to the renowned 19th-century Polish actress Helena Modrzejewska at the entrance. A service dedicated to the city's thespians is held here at 10.30am every Sunday.

Below: details of Florian's Gate.

The Piarists' Church Crypt

Every year during Holy Week a reproduction of Christ's Tomb is set up in the crypt of the Piarists' Church. The crypt is also sometimes a venue for exhibitions and theatre performances.

features a royal Polish eagle of the Piast dynasty designed by Matejko.

The passageway within the gate features a small, mid-19th century altar around a Gothic painting of Our Lady Mary of Piaski. A section of the historic city wall, together with four bastions dating from the 14th century, extend on either side of Florian's Gate. This wall now serves as open-air exhibition space for local painters (whose range covers the usual spectrum, from genuinely artistic to downright kitsch).

PIARISTS' CHURCH

Continue along ul. Pijarska. By the junction with ul. św Jana is the **Piarists' Church** ❻ (Kościół Pijarów), one of the city's smallest and most fascinating churches. The Piarist Order first built a chapel and adjoining residence in Krakow in 1682, after the brothers had been asked to teach students of theology at the Jagiellonian University. The con-gregation grew to the extent that the chapel soon became too small, so Duke Hieronim Lubomirski acquired a neighbouring disused brewery for the Piarists. Wealthy Cracovians contributed to the building costs, and the new church was consecrated in 1728.

The interiors feature Franciszek Eckstein and Jakub Hoffman's highly effective illusionistic murals, modelled on those of St Ignatius' Church in Rome, while the vaulted ceiling and a depiction of Christ Ascending into Heaven (copied from Raphael) by the altar are particularly impressive.

Should you wish to eat before heading any further, try the **Chłopskie Jadło**, see ⊕②, two minutes south along ul. św Jana on the corner of ul. św Marka.

CZARTORYSKI MUSEUM

Opposite the Piarists' Church is one of the city's most important museums, **Czartoryski Museum** ❼ (Muzeum Czartoryskich; ul. św Jana 19; tel: 012 422 55 66; www.muzeum-czartorys kich.krakow.pl; May–Oct Tue, Thur 10am–4pm, Wed, Fri–Sat 10am–7pm, Sun 10am–3pm; Nov–Apr Tue, Thur, Sun 10am–3.30pm, Wed, Fri–Sat 10am–6pm; charge). This historic palace and the neighbouring monastery were acquired by the Czartoryski family in 1876 to display their magnificent art collection. The municipality donated the adjoining Renaissance arsenal to provide further galleries (used for temporary exhibitions). These buildings offer a period setting for a fine collection that includes Polish and other

---

Food and Drink

② CHŁOPSKIE JADŁO

Ul. św Jana 3; tel: 012 429 51 57; daily noon–11pm; €€€
The Peasant's Kitchen evokes the traditional spirit of Polish-style hospitality in a wonderful replica of a 19th-century country inn. Fine country cooking includes the likes of *bigos* (hunter's stew, comprising five different types of meat simmered with mushrooms, cabbage and sauerkraut), and *golonka* (pork cooked in beer) served with mustard and horseradish. Live folk music.

③ POLSKIE JADŁO COMPENDIUM CULINARIUM

Ul. św Jana 30; tel: 012 433 98 25; daily noon–11pm; €€€€
It's the live music and oom-pah-pah atmosphere as opposed to the food that keeps people coming back here. There's a band – usually brought in from some remote mountain village – almost every night, who make a loud accompaniment to your food: a regular mix of game dishes served in huge portions.

European paintings, sculpture, sacral art and objets d'art, as well as ancient Roman, Greek and Egyptian art.

The Painting Gallery

Featuring 13th- to 16th-century Polish, German, Italian, Spanish, Flemish and Dutch masters, the highlights here are Rembrandt's *Landscape with a Merciful Samaritan* painted in 1638, and Leonardo da Vinci's *Lady with an Ermine* (1480–90). This captivating, enigmatic portrait, thought to be of an Italian duke's mistress, was purchased by the Czartoryski family in 1800.

The Tent Room

The Tent Room's collection of Turkish effects was acquired at the Battle of Vienna in 1683, when King Jan III Sobieski led the victorious charge against the Ottoman aggressors. This exhibition includes a magnificent Turkish pavilion, suits of armour, various military items and even coffee cups (the first coffee imbibed in Poland was taken from Turkish pavilions by the king).

Opposite the museum on ul. św Jana is the **Compendium Culinarium**, a good choice for a long lunch, see ⑪③.

CHURCH OF THE STS JOHN

Head south along ul. św Jana. On the left, just before ul. św Tomasza, is the **Church of St John the Baptist and St John the Evangelist ❽** (Kościół św Jana Chrzciciela i św Jana Ewangelisty). While the foundations and crypt of the original 12th-century Romanesque church have survived, the

predominantly Baroque characteristics derive from the 17th century. The Baroque side altars in black and gold form a vivid contrast with the otherwise plain white interiors.

Adjacent to the main altar is a painting of *Matka Bożej od Wykupu Niewolników* (Holy Mary Mother of God, of Releasing Prisoners of War) also known as *Matka Boska Wolności* (Holy Mary Mother of God of Liberty), which was donated by Duke Stanisław Radziwiłł – who acquired it in Spain – in about 1577. Since the early 17th century, this painting has been associated with those Polish prisoners of war who were 'miraculously' freed after being sentenced to death by the Ottomans. The handcuffs of one such liberated prisoner still hang by the painting. King Jan III Sobieski, who defeated the Turks at the Battle of Vienna, subsequently prayed here in 1684 as a token of gratitude.

Continue along ul. św Jana to return to Main Market Square.

Above from far left: the passageway within Florian's Gate has a small altar and gives a view of the Barbican; a door handle and the façade of the Piarists' Church; gallery in the Czartoryski Museum.

Lady with an Ermine The Czartoryski Museum's prize exhibit, Leonardo da Vinci's *Lady with an Ermine* (pictured left), was hidden from the Nazis at the outbreak of World War II, only to be found and made part of Hitler's personal art collection. It was returned to Krakow in 1946.

WAWEL

Before there was Krakow there was Wawel, and this tour takes in both the royal castle and the cathedral, including the sumptuously furnished apartments that once accommodated Poland's kings.

Timing your Visit
To get the best out of Wawel, arrive early. Begin your day with the Royal Apartments tour before exploring the rest of the castle, the cathedral and then the grounds. To see everything properly you will need a full day.

Food Options
There are now no restaurants up on the hill, and the few kiosks on the way up are notorious for charging small fortunes for a bottle of water. Bring plenty of liquid refreshment, a packed lunch, or be prepared to make your way down to the nearest restaurants down the hill; you could try Smak Ukrainski on ul. Kanonicza for example *(see* ⑪① *on p.40).*

DISTANCE N/A – the tour is spent in the grounds of Wawel
TIME A full day
START Wawel Castle
END Dragon's Cave
POINTS TO NOTE

Access Wawel via a cobbled route leading up from Podzamcze. You emerge into a large square with the main tourist office to your right; this is the only place in the city where you can buy tickets for Wawel. Tickets for the cathedral must be bought from a separate ticket office opposite the cathedral entrance. Visitor numbers are restricted, and entry to some of the sites operates on a timed basis. Tickets can sell out early in the day during peak season; to reserve in advance tel: 012 422 51 55 ext. 291 or 012 422 1697. Collect your tickets from the main Wawel ticket office at least 20 minutes before the reserved time. See www.wawel.krakow.pl.

Wawel Castle and **Cathedral** tower over a 25-m (80-ft) high limestone hill overlooking the Wisła (Vistula) River. In the words of Stanisław Wyspiański: 'Here everything is Poland, every stone and fragment, and the person who enters here becomes a part of Poland.'

Royal Residence
Wawel Hill was established as the royal residence in 1038 when King Kazimierz Odnowiciel (Casimir the Restorer) transplanted the capital from Gniezno to Krakow and began building a royal residence. Under King Kazimierz Wielki (Casimir the Great, 1333–70) this evolved into a Gothic castle complex with defensive walls and towers that was subsequently extended by King Władysław Jagiełło (1386–1434).

Fire and Reconstruction
The castle was ravaged by fire in 1499 but some of its Gothic elements, such as the Kurza Stopa (Hen's Foot Tower), survived and were incorporated into a larger castle built by King Zygmunt Stary in 1506–35. He wanted a palatial residence and he certainly succeeded in creating one. The castle's perfectly proportioned, three-storey, arcaded courtyard is one of Europe's finest examples of Renaissance architecture. The designs were initiated by the Italian architect Francisco the Florentine and, in 1516, continued by another Italian architect, Bartolomeo Berrecci. The castle was finished in 1536, but subsequent fires meant refurbishment was required; in 1595, Giovanni Trevano introduced the early Baroque elements and two additional towers.

Warsaw was declared the capital of Poland in 1596, and King Zygmunt III Waza (1587–1632) transferred the royal residence to Warsaw's Royal Castle in 1609. Though Wawel's importance was diminishing, it remained the site of the royal treasury and continued to hold coronations and royal funerals.

Invasion of the Swedes

Wawel was ravaged and looted during the Swedish invasion of 1665–7, and the castle was torched by Swedish soldiers in 1702. In the 1780s, King Stanisław August Poniatowski commissioned his favourite architect, the Italian Dominik Merlini, to oversee the refurbishments, introducing neoclassical elements. The partitions of Poland at the end of the 18th century saw the Prussians and then the Austrians loot the royal treasury. Austria turned the castle into a military barracks.

20th-Century Wawel

It wasn't until 1905 that Austrian troops left the castle and renovation work could be started. Work was still in progress when the Germans invaded in 1939. The main body of the castle had opened as a museum when Poland regained independence in 1918. Many of the castle's treasures were shipped to Canada during the first few days of the invasion, thus denying the Nazis some handsome booty. Hans Frank, governor general of the puppet government, subsequently established his headquarters within Wawel. The castle and cathedral became a museum in 1945.

WAWEL CASTLE

From the main Wawel courtyard, walk past the cathedral and through the small alleyway which leads into a second courtyard, known as the Castle Courtyard. In the far, southeastern corner is the entrance to the **State Rooms and Royal Private Apartments** (Reprezentacyjne Komnaty i Prywatne Apartamenty Królewskie; Apr–Oct Tue, Fri 9.30am–5pm, Wed, Thur, Sat 9.30am–4pm, Sun 10am–4pm; Nov–Mar Tue–Sat 9.30am–3pm; State Rooms also Apr–Oct Mon 9.30am–1pm. Admission to Royal Private Apartments in groups of up to 10, guided tours only, fee includes guide service).

State Rooms

The castle's **State Rooms** ❶ (Komnaty Królewskie), spread over the ground and second floors, may be viewed without a guide, though it is

Above from far left:
Wawel Castle and Cathedral; in the castle courtyard.

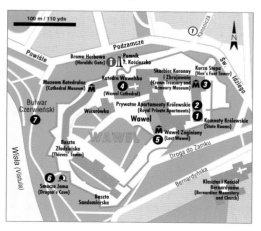

Wawel Acropolis

In 1905 Stanisław Wyspiański *(see p.73)* came up with ambitious plans to remodel Wawel along neoclassical lines, creating what he called the Wawel Acropolis; only his death prevented him from carrying out the work. A model of how Wawel might have looked can be seen in the Wyspiański Museum *(see p.71)*.

Below: the cathedral blends a number of architectural styles.

best to follow the 'suggested' route. This takes you through the former **Governor's Suite** on the ground floor, the highlight of which is the reception room, whose original 16th-century furniture and décor remain. The Baroque tapestries which adorn the walls are of particular note. Climbing the **Deputies' Staircase** to the second floor, you will emerge in the Tournament Hall, which has impressive Italian furniture brought from Siena.

The adjoining **Audience Hall** (Sala Poselska) is perhaps the most famous in the castle. Also known as **Hall under the Heads** (Sala Pod Głowami), the ceiling is adorned with 30 sculpted heads of kings, knights, burghers and allegorical and mythical figures; the 30 heads are all that remain of 194 originally commissioned by Zygmunt Stary.

Walk back past the staircase to the **Hall under the Eagle** (Sala Pod Orłem), in which hang many fine royal portraits, such as Rubens's *Elizabeth of Bourbon* (1629), while the **Hall Under the Birds** (Sala Pod Ptakami) features bird sculptures and a frieze that includes birds in its motifs. This is where King Zygmunt III Waza received foreign delegations – you can see the royal crest on a 16th-century wall-hanging and on the stone portal.

Next door is the castle's largest hall, the **Senators' Hall** (Sala Senatorska), which served as the home of the Senate. It now displays an impressive arras (tapestry) entitled *Cain Kills Abel*. This is one of a magnificent collection of wall-hangings – initially commissioned in the mid-16th century by King Zyg-

munt Stary and later by his son, King Zygmunt August – which are displayed throughout the castle. Produced in Brussels, the series is divided into three themes: Old Testament scenes, animals in exotic landscapes, and royal crests and insignia. Of the original 360 arrases, only 142 survived the Nazis.

Royal Private Apartments

On leaving the Senators' Hall, you need to return to the ground floor to pick up the guided tour of the sumptuous **Royal Private Apartments** ❷ (Prywatne Apartamenty Królewskie), which are in fact located on the first floor. The tour passes through various Renaissance and Baroque apartments, including the **King's Suite**, of which the highlight is his office, featuring rich 16th-century stucco decoration. Two dark, windowless rooms lead off from here, in the so-called **Hen's Foot Tower**: their purpose is unknown, but they may well have been prisons.

The **Guest Bedroom**, the last room on the tour, features the oldest tapestry in the castle, from the 15th century, and a late Renaissance English-style fireplace. The Italian paintings on the walls are all part of the magnificent **Lanckoroński Collection**, which once decorated the Lanckoroński Palace in Vienna (the Lanckorońskis were a wealthy Cracovian family who relocated to Vienna after the partition of Poland in 1795). After the fall of Communism in Poland, the Countess Karolina Lanckorońska donated the collection to the Wawel museum authorities.

Treasury and Armoury

After you leave the State Rooms and Royal Private Apartments, the entrance to the **Crown Treasury and Armoury Museum** ❸ (Skarbiec Koronny i Zbrojownia; Apr–Oct Tue, Fri 9.30am–5pm, Wed, Thur, Sat 9.30am–4pm, Sun 10am–4pm, Mon 9.30am–1pm; Nov–Mar Tue–Sat 9.30am–3pm; charge) is found to your right, on the same side of the courtyard. It is housed in a Gothic section of the castle, complete with vaulted ceilings. The 13th-century *szczerbiec* ('jagged sword'), used at Polish coronations from 1320, is one of the most important exhibits of coronation regalia, royal jewels and medieval sacral art. Among the suits of armour and weapons are some ferocious double-handed swords, and the winged suits of armour worn by Polish hussars at the Battle of Vienna in 1683.

The **Museum of Oriental Art** (Sztuka Wschodu; Apr–Oct Tue, Fri 9.30am–5pm, Wed, Thur, Sat 9.30am–4pm, Sun 10am–3pm; Nov–Mar Tue–Sat noon–3pm; charge) brings together Turkish pavilions, armour, rugs and porcelain, some of which was taken as booty after the Battle of Vienna.

WAWEL CATHEDRAL

As the scene of royal coronations, weddings, funerals and state occasions, **Wawel Cathedral** ❹ (Katedra Wawelska; May–Sept Mon–Sat 9am–5pm, Sun and holidays 12.15–5pm; Oct–Apr 9am–3pm) is Poland's most important church. A set of prehistoric bones by the entrance portal (designed by Trevano)

has hung here for centuries. Local superstition holds that the bones are those of a dragon that inhabited a cave beneath the castle, from which it terrorised the city; only while the bones remain in place will the cathedral be safe. The scientific verdict links the 'dragon's bones' to prehistoric mammals.

The Interior

The cathedral was built on the site of two Romanesque churches. It blends Gothic, Renaissance and Baroque, but also has some Seccessionist stained-glass windows by Józef Mehoffer. Entering through the main entrance, ahead of you is the Baroque main altar, which dates from the mid-17th century and features an emotive painting of the Crucifixion.

Taking a clockwise route around the cathedral you will pass a total of 18 impressive side chapels dating from the 14th to 18th centuries, including **Holy Cross Chapel** (Kaplica Świętokrzyska),

Above from far left:
stained-glass window in the cathedral; there's a lot to see inside the cathedral.

Below: the cathedral's spires.

Manga Museum

Across the river from Wawel is Manggha, Krakow's Museum of Japanese Art and Technology, consisting mainly of the astonishing, absorbing collection of Feliks Jasienski (1861–1929) a legendary Cracovian adventurer. To get to it, take tram no. 18 three stops from the Wawel stop (on the corner of Stradom and św Gertrudy) to Most Grunwaldzki.

whose remarkable frescoes incorporate Ruthenian and Byzantine elements. The most spectacular chapel, **Sigismund's Chapel** (Kaplica Zygmuntowska, 1519–33), was designed by Santi Gucci, Padovano and Berreccio, and is regarded as one of the finest examples of Renaissance sacral art in Europe. Crowned by a gilded dome, using a mere 50kg (110lbs) of gold leaf, the chapel is the Jagiellonian dynasty's mausoleum. The tomb of King Zygmunt August is a masterpiece in red marble. It is the fourth chapel on the right-hand side of the cathedral.

Royal Tombs

At the head of the church is the **Stefan Batory Chapel**, opposite which are the **royal tombs**. The earliest is the sarcophagus of King Władysław Łokietek (1333). The highly ornate tomb of St Stanisław, Poland's patron saint, with bas-reliefs depicting his life, dates from 1671 and was sculpted in Gdańsk. The bishop was murdered in 1079 on the orders of King Boleslaus the Bold, who didn't appreciate the bishop's criticisms of his immoral lifestyle.

Opposite, in a Baroque altar from 1745, is the **Cross with the Black Christ** (Gothic Krzyż z Czarnym

Chrystusem). It was brought to Poland by Queen Jadwiga, who left her native Hungary in 1384 aged 14. She was canonised by Pope John Paul II in 1997 for her endless charitable work and for promoting Catholicism in Poland.

The Crypt

More royal tombs, as well as those of renowned Poles such as the poets Adam Mickiewicz and Juliusz Słowacki, Tadeusz Kościuszko (who led the 1794 uprising during the partition of Poland), and the 20th-century statesman Marshal Józef Piłsudski, can be seen in the **crypt**, accessed via an entrance to the left of the main altar. This is usually far less crowded than the main cathedral and on hot summer afternoons is a reflective, cooling place.

The first section, known as St Leonard's Crypt, is a prime example of Romanesque style. This is where the newly ordained Fr Karol Wojtyła (subsequently Pope John Paul II) celebrated his first Mass on 2 November 1946. As Bishop of Krakow he presided over Wawel Cathedral for 10 years.

Sigismund's Bell

The remarkable **Sigismund's Bell** (Dzwon Zygmunta) is in the cathedral's **Sigismund's Tower** (Wieża Zygmuntowska; same times as cathedral; charge). Cast in 1520 and hung the next year, the bell weighs 18 tonnes. It's the largest bell in Poland, and is rung only on special occasions. The climb up the tower's steep, cramped staircase is hard work, but definitely worthwhile. According to superstition, touch the

Food and Drink

① SMAK UKRAINSKI

Ul. Kanonicza 15; tel: 012 421 92 94; noon–9.30pm; €€€
In winter the cellars of this 16th-century house make a great place for warming portions of *żarke*, a Ukrainian beef stew. In summer the garden is an equally great place to dine, and at any time of the year, friendly staff in Ukrainian national dress keep you plied with bottles of sweet Soviet champagne.

bell's clapper with your left hand and your wish will be granted. There are also fabulous views over the historic centre.

Cathedral Museum

Opposite the cathedral entrance, a separate building houses the **Cathedral Museum** (Muzeum Katedralne; Tue–Sun 10am–3pm; charge), an initiative of the pope when he was Bishop of Krakow. Here you can see 12th- to 18th-century sacral art, rugs, votive offerings and religious relics.

LOST WAWEL

To the right of the cathedral, housed within the former royal kitchens and coach house, **Lost Wawel** ❺ (Wawel Zaginiony; Apr–Oct Mon 9.30am–noon, Tue–Thur 9.30am–4pm, Fri–Sun 9.30am–3pm; Nov–Mar Mon–Sat 9.30am–3pm, Sun 10am–3pm; charge) includes archaeological and architectural remains, such as decorative Gothic tiles and the poignant rotunda of the Church of the Blessed Virgin Mary, one of the earliest buildings on Wawel Hill. Outside are well-preserved parts of the 15th- to 16th-century defensive walls, as well as some medieval ruins.

DRAGON'S CAVE

At the far end of the castle grounds (walk towards the Baszta Sandomierska exit) are the steps which lead down to the **Dragon's Cave** ❻ (Smocza Jama; daily Apr–June, Sept, Oct 10am–5pm; July–Aug 10am–6pm; charge) is thought to be one of several

under Wawel Hill and has been the scene of many a licentious episode. In the 19th century it housed a brothel, until the Austrian authorities bricked up the cave entrance. At the exit, a metal sculpture of a slim dragon periodically breathes gas flames.

BY THE RIVER

Between Wawel and the Wisła is a small strip of parkland by the river known as **Bulwar Czerwieński** ❼, which is popular in the summer with the locals as a place to lie in the sun and do nothing, and where you can join boat trips along the river. In the high season, boats moored by the river sell food and drink.

King Krak

The legend of the dragon has numerous variations. One constant theme finds the dragon woken from sleep by the noise of the castle's builders. Venturing out for food, the dragon devours beautiful virgins, handsome young men, and any creature it comes across. Some versions claim that King Krak delivered his people from the dragon, others that he sought a volunteer – promising half the kingdom and his daughter's hand in marriage – to slay the beast. Many knights tried and failed. Eventually a shoemaker left a sheep's carcass filled with sulphur and salt by the cave entrance. Either the contents of the sheep made the dragon so thirsty that it drank until it burst, or the sheep blew up inside it. The shoemaker married the princess, and they lived happily ever after.

KAZIMIERZ

Explore Kazimierz, the historic Jewish district of Krakow, taking in an array of synagogues from different periods, a number of Jewish museums and cultural centres, and a host of Jewish cafés and restaurants.

Staying in Kazimierz
Kazimierz is as lively during the evening – if not more so – as it is during the day. For the full Kazimierz experience, you can stay in one of the area's hotels; there are more than 10 to choose from, some catering to Jews and offering a full kosher package *(see p.115)*.

DISTANCE 2km (1 mile)
TIME A full day
START Tempel Synagogue
END New Jewish Cemetery
POINTS TO NOTE
Kazimierz is easy to reach from Main Market Square – walk along ul. Grodzka, then take ul. Stradomska and turn into ul. Miodowa. On completing the route, walk back under the railway bridge to ul. Starowiślna, and take either tram no. 9 or no. 13 back towards the city centre.

You can start your walk with cake, sandwiches, tea or coffee (or something a little stronger) at the **8 Day Café** at Podbrzezie 4, just past the Tempel Synagogue, see ⑪①.

Kazimierz was founded as a town in its own right just outside Krakow by King Kazimierz Wielki (Casimir the Great), who gave the town his own name, in 1335. Although Kazimierz is known as a centre of Jewish life, it was not totally so – the district has several historic Roman Catholic churches. The Jewish nature of Kazimierz dates back to 1494 and King

Schindler's List
Though the film *Schindler's List* was mainly set in the Nazi-created ghetto of Podgórze *(see p.82)*, most of the film was actually shot on the streets of Kazimierz. The courtyard at ul. Józefa 12 features prominently in the early part of the film.

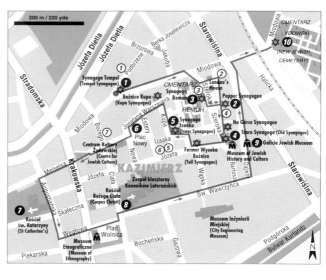

Jan Olbracht's expulsion of Krakow's Jewish population. Many settled in Kazimierz, to which they were followed by other persecuted Jews from across Europe.

Flourishing Community

Commerce thrived and, by the 16th century, the town's Jewish community was one of the most prominent in Europe. Indeed the renowned Talmudic scholar and philosopher Rabbi Moses Isserles (known as Remuh) founded his academy here. Kazimierz became a walled town, complete with gateways, town hall and market place in the early 17th century. Only in 1800, when this part of Poland was annexed by the Austro-Hungarian Empire, was Kazimierz incorporated into Krakow.

The Holocaust

When Germany invaded Poland in September 1939, about 70,000 Jews lived in Kazimierz, most of whom were soon 'resettled' in other parts of the country. In 1941 the Nazis established a Jewish ghetto in Podgórze, a separate district of Krakow (see p.80), into which they herded Kazimierz's remaining 20,000 Jews. Yet unlike so many of the Continent's centres of Jewish life, Kazimierz survived – the Nazis planned to establish a macabre museum of what were termed 'vanished races' in this area.

TEMPEL SYNAGOGUE

At the junction of ul. Podbrzezie and ul. Miodowa you'll find the Reform (as opposed to Orthodox) Jewish congregation's **Tempel Synagogue** ❶ (ul. Miodowa 24; tel: 012 429 57 35; Sun–Fri 9am-4pm; charge). This synagogue was built in 1862, and extended on both sides in 1924. Of the few houses of Jewish prayer in Kazimierz that survived the Nazi regime virtually intact, this was the newest.

Beautiful Interior

Whereas the façade combines neo-Renaissance with Moorish influences, the interiors blend beautifully ornate stucco work, intricate red-and-gold polychromy, and a set of four circular stained-glass windows by the altar closet. Above highly gilded galleries on both sides, the beautiful ceiling is decorated with gold stars on a light-blue background. An exhibition area includes photographs and architectural drawings of all the synagogues in Kazimierz, together with historical details.

Further ahead, across the road, beyond a courtyard, you can see the rear elevation of the 17th-century **Kupa Synagogue** (Bożnica Kupa). The front of this building is on ul. Warszauera.

Food and Drink 🍴

① 8 DAY CAFE
Ul. Podbrzezie 4; no telephone; 9am–10pm; €€
Renovated in 2008 with bright colours giving it a positively Mediterranean feel, this lively café remains a favourite of locals and visitors alike. Good coffee and a great selection of pastries make it an ideal place to fuel up for the day.

Above from far left: a row of recreated shopfronts relating to early 20th-century Jewish traders disguises Dawno Temu na Kazimierzu restaurant within (see p.122); the Star of David in the Tempel Synagogue; Noah's Ark restaurant (see p.122); the ornate interior of Tempel Synagogue.

Below: details from Tempel Synagogue.

WIDE STREET

Continue past ul. Jakuba and turn right into **ul. Szeroka** (Wide Street) and you will be in what was once Kazimierz's centre of Jewish life and commerce. There was a time when this quiet neighbourhood was the most prestigious residential street inhabited by the wealthiest Jews. Restoration work has preserved its Jewish character. Growing numbers of tourists take 'Oskar Schindler tours' *(see margin on p.42)*, and wandering troubadors play nostalgic tunes in the Jewish cafés and restaurants.

Food and Drink

② KLEZMER-HOIS
Ul. Szeroka 6; tel: 012 411 12 45; daily 10am–10pm; €€€
The hotel café has the air of a bourgeois home – oil paintings, vases with roses on each table, and comfortable sofas and armchairs make for a very pleasant scene. The restaurant manages to be more formal and more stylishly bohemian at the same time. Jewish and Polish dishes include excellent *chłodnik* (cold beetroot soup with sour cream and dill) and baked cheesecake.

③ SZARA KAZIMIERZ
Ul. Szeroka 39; tel: 012 429 12 19; daily 11am–11pm; €€€
A mainstay of Main Market Square *(see p.120)*, Szara has branched out into Kazimierz. This restaurant offers something different from the standard Jewish fare of the area, with an interesting menu of modern European food and some sensational fusion dishes that combine seafood and traditional Polish cuisine. Add in smart, polite staff and decent – though not cheap – prices, and you have a great place for lunch or dinner.

④ ARIEL
Ul. Szeroka 18; tel: 012 421 79 20; daily 10am–midnight; €€€
Choose from pavement tables overlooking the street, a sheltered patio courtyard with a goldfish pond, or the conservative, 1970s-style dining room with paintings depicting Jewish life. There's also plenty of choice on the Polish/Jewish menu, with classics such as herring fillets in sour cream, chicken soup and *pierogi* (ravioli) stuffed with curd cheese. A small bookshop in the entrance hall sells guidebooks and souvenirs from Kazimierz.

Landau's House

The substantial **Landau's House** (at no. 2) was built as a manor house in the 16th century by the wealthy magnate and Kazimierz worthy Spytko Jordan. Overlooking a small green, it now houses the Jarden bookshop, which stocks a good range of guidebooks. Check out the attractive, 1920s-style décor of the Noah's Ark café and, if you fancy expert accompaniment to your visit, this is the place to book local Jewish guides for walking tours of the area.

Also dating from the 16th century, the **Klezmer-Hois Hotel and Café** (no. 6; see ⑪②) occupies a building that used to house the *mikve* (ritual baths).

Popper Synagogue

The **Popper Synagogue** ②, approached through a courtyard at no. 16, was founded in 1620 by Wolf Popper, a wealthy merchant and financier also known as Bocian ('Stork'). Originally decorated and furnished in a lavish style, it was destroyed by the Nazis and is currently used as a cultural centre.

REMUH SYNAGOGUE

Working your way back up the opposite side of the street, the smallest synagogue in Kazimierz, **Remuh** ③ (ul. Szeroka 40; Sun–Fri 9am–4pm; charge) is not merely a historic monument: it remains the centre of the neighbourhood's Jewish life and has an active, albeit small, congregation. Remuh, which dates from 1558, was the town's second synagogue, and was

originally known as the 'New Synagogue'. The founder, Israel ben Joseph, was a merchant and banker to King Zygmunt Stary, and the father of the renowned rabbi and philosopher Remuh (1525–72).

Approach the synagogue via a small, irregular courtyard and you'll see a harmonious blend of architectural genres. The current appearance dates from the major refurbishment of the 1820s and the post-war reconstruction. A rectangular, single-aisle hall is overlooked by a women's gallery. The stone money box by the entrance to the prayer room dates from the 16th century, while the altar features a plaque commemorating the spot where Rabbi Remuh prayed, and there are Renaissance stone portal and Secessionist doors. Caramel-coloured walls provide a background for fragments of period tiles with classical motifs, and a few early 20th-century wall paintings depict Noah's Ark, the grave of the biblical matriarch Rachel and Jerusalem's Wailing Wall.

Renaissance Cemetery

There is also a Wailing Wall in the adjoining **cemetery**, on the ul. Szeroka side. This was built with fragments of Nazi-desecrated tombstones that were too small to be reconstructed. This, one of two Renaissance Jewish cemeteries in Europe (the other is in Prague), was laid out in the 1530s and was active until the early 19th century. Some 700 gravestones, including ornate Renaissance and baroque examples, fill 4.5 ha (11 acres). If you're ready for a coffee or lunch break, try **Szara Kazimierz** beside the synagogue at no. 39, see ⑪③, or **Ariel** restaurant at no. 18, see ⑪④.

OLD SYNAGOGUE

At the southern end of the street is Poland's oldest surviving synagogue, **Old Synagogue** ❹ (Stara Synagoga; ul. Szeroka 24; tel: 012 422 09 62; Apr–Oct Mon 10am–2pm, Tue–Sun 10am–5pm; Nov–Mar Wed, Thur, Sat, Sun 9am–4pm, Mon 10am–2pm, Fri 10am–5pm; charge), home to the **Museum of Jewish History and Culture**. Dating from the early 15th century, this building was partly modelled on synagogues in Prague, Regensburg and Worms, which explains the Gothic façade. It was extended in the 16th century, when the architect Matteo Gucci of Florence introduced the synagogue's Renaissance elements. In the following century, a women's prayer room and a meeting hall for the Jewish Community Council were established on the first floor. Demolition work in 1880 revealed some of the synagogue's original walls. Based on this discovery, reconstruction combined the original style with neo-Renaissance elements. The rebuilding process continued until the early 20th century; the synagogue remained the centre of Jewish worship in Kazimierz until the Nazi invasion. The Nazis used it as a warehouse before destroying the interiors and roof. It wasn't until several years after the war that the ruins were reconstructed. The synagogue reopened as a museum in 1958.

Above from far left: Museum of Jewish History and Culture in the Old Synagogue; the Remuh Synagogue's Wailing Wall; the synagogue dates back to 1558.

Below: gravestones in the Remuh Synagogue's cemetery.

Joseph Street

Ul. Józefa takes its name not from the biblical Joseph but from Habsburg Emperor Joseph II, who enjoyed staying in Kazimierz while touring his eastern territories.

Museum of Jewish History and Culture

The museum's extensive collection provides such good explanations of the Jewish faith, its history and culture that, even if you have little prior knowledge, it is easy to understand the significance of each exhibit. Numerous religious items were collected from other synagogues. The main picture gallery includes portraits by the renowned painter Józef Mehoffer, whereas the gallery on the first floor features 19th- and early 20th-century views of Kazimierz. An exhibition of Jewish life in Kazimierz 1939–45 displays original photographs and documents that trace the course of the Nazi regime, taking in the ghetto and subsequent transports to concentration camps.

A monument in front of the museum marks the site where 30 Polish men and boys were executed by Nazis in 1943.

TWO FORMER SYNAGOGUES

To the left of the Old Synagogue is the former **Na Górce Synagogue**. Though the name's literal translation is 'Synagogue on the Hill', it actually means 'Upper Synagogue', signifying that the prayer hall was on the first floor (the ground floor housed a *mikve*). This synagogue was known for its connection with Natan Spira, who lectured across Europe on the practice of Kabbala (a mystical means of understanding the Old Testament).

Tall Synagogue

Leave ul. Szeroka by the southwestern corner and head along ul. Józefa where you will find the former **Tall Synagogue** (Wysoka Bożnica; no. 38) on the right, dating from the mid-16th century and restored after its destruction by the Nazis in 1939. The façade features a Renaissance portal and four elegant buttresses. As at Na Górce, the prayer hall was on the first floor. The building now houses a branch of the city's conservation department and a bookshop.

Latin American Lunch Options

A short (50 m/yd) detour can be made from here to Józefa no. 26, where two heavily competing Latin American restaurants stand side by side: Cuban **Buena Vista** and upmarket **Pimiento**, see ⑪⑤ and ⑪⑥.

Kazimierz's Revival

From the end of World War II until Poland's return to democracy in 1989, Kazimierz was one of the most deprived and indeed dangerous areas of Krakow. Since 1989, however, Polish Jews who had emigrated to Israel have been free to return to the area either to reclaim confiscated property or simply to invest, and have driven a remarkable turnaround in fortunes. Cheap property prices at the beginning of the 1990s encouraged young Polish entrepreneurs to set up shop here, either as bar and restaurant owners or shopkeepers. Students – attracted by cheap rents – soon followed. Add the lively cultural scene – which grew up around the resurrected Judaic Cultural Centre – and the area was already blooming long before Steven Spielberg really put it on the map in the film *Schindler's List*. While property prices are now among the highest in Krakow, the area is still popular with students and has retained its bohemian character.

ISAAC SYNAGOGUE

Just after the Tall Synagogue turn right into ul. Jakuba (Jacob Street), which leads directly to ul. Izaaka (Isaac Street; *see margin right*). Ceremoniously inaugurated in 1644, the **Isaac Synagogue** ❺ (ul. Kupa 18; Sun–Fri 9am–6pm; charge) is the largest synagogue in Kazimierz, and was, in contrast with its current minimalist interiors, also the most lavishly furnished. Ravaged by the Nazis, the building served as a sculptor's workshop after the war, and it wasn't until 1983 that renovation work began. Nevertheless, the Baroque prayer hall retains a distinctive beauty and features fragments of recently uncovered 17th-century wall murals together with some stucco decoration by Giovanni Battista

Falconi. On the east wall is a stone altar tabernacle *(aron hakodesh)*; the women's gallery *(ezrat nashim)* features an elegant arcade of Tuscan columns. Cardboard figures represent rabbis, and a small television screens a short historical film about the Jews of Kazimierz. In another part of the synagogue, adjoining a photographic exhibition of pre-war life entitled 'The Memory of Polish Jews', you can see a film by the American Julian Bryan that traces the history of Jewish life in Krakow and Kazimierz.

NEW SQUARE

Turn right on leaving the synagogue, on to ul. Kupa, and walk towards the **Kupa Synagogue** (Bożnica Kupa) at the end of the street. Take a left here

Food and Drink 🍴

❺ BUENA VISTA
Ul. Józefa 26; tel: 066 803 50 00; daily noon–11.30pm; €€€€
The most cosmopolitan restaurant in Kazimierz, and the first to offer a real alternative to Jewish/kosher food. You can feast on a whole range of Cuban treats, including Cuban gazpacho and chicken in Jerez sauce with lemon. Separate bar area serves great Latino cocktails too.

❻ PIMIENTO
Ul. Józefa 26; tel: 012 421 25 02; daily noon–11pm; €€€€€
Expensive this place may be, but there is a reason for that: all of the hardware (that being the beef) is imported direct from Argentina. As such you are guaranteed a sensational, enormous steak that will both look and taste fit for a gaucho.

Above from far left: shady outdoor café; the Tall Synagogue's altar for holding the Torah; the Isaac Synagogue; an elder resident of Kazimierz.

Isaac Street
Ul. Izaaka was named after Yitzhok ben Yekeles (Isaac, son of Jacob), one of 17th-century Kazimierz's wealthiest merchants and moneylenders and founder of the Isaac Synagogue.

Left: the Tall Synagogue; **below:** Plac Nowy is the venue for a fruit and vegetable market.

City Engineering Museum

Housed in an old tram depot at ul. św Wawrzyńca 15, the City Engineering Museum (Museum Inżynierii Miejskiej; Tue–Sun 10am-4pm; charge) is at once both a fascinating history of public transport in Krakow and a collection of hands-on exhibits aimed at encouraging children to become interested in engineering.

Below: traditional moccasins and belt, and old paintings, in the Ethnographic Museum.

on to ul. Warszauera and continue for 100 metres/yds into **Plac Nowy** ❻ (New Square). A small, circular building occupies its centre, which is the tiled interior of the old fruit and vegetable market. The square with its bric-a-brac and hot food stalls has been revived by an influx of cafés and bars *(see p.46)*, but retains an edgy individuality.

CENTRE FOR JEWISH CULTURE

Cross over to the **Centrum Kultury Żydowskiej** (Judaica Foundation, Centre for Jewish Culture; ul. Meiselsa 17; tel: 012 430 64 49; Mon–Fri 10am–6pm, Sat–Sun 10am–2pm). Established in 1993 and concealed behind the 1886 period façade of the former B'ne Emuna prayer house, the centre's motto, L'dor v'dor (Hebrew for 'from generation to generation'), emphasises its commitment to Jewish culture and continuity after the Holocaust. There is a yearly Festival of Jewish Culture, and the centre also incorporates a workshop, an art gallery, a bookshop that sells antique books and postcards, and a café.

Futher along ul. Meiselsa and a right turn on ul. Bożego Ciała will lead you to **Enzo** at no. 14, see ⑪⑦, a cool café and night-time hangout.

ST CATHERINE'S CHURCH

Continue along ul. Meiselsa and turn left into ul. Augustiańska, which leads to **Kościół św Katarzyny** ❼ (St Catherine's Church; no. 7). This prime example of Gothic architecture was founded by King Kazimierz Wielki in 1363, apparently as a form of penance for sentencing Fr Marcin Baryczka to death by drowning in the River Vistula. This was a classic case of shooting the messenger: the priest had committed the heinous crime of conveying the bishop's disapproval of the king's dalliances with various mistresses.

The church's interiors include Baroque details, such as the impressive altar. The cloisters of the adjoining Augustinian monastery feature remarkable frescoes from the 14th and 15th centuries. An altar dedicated to Matka Boska Pocieszenia (Our Lady the Comforter) was one of the most important sites in Poland's cult of the Virgin Mary.

ETHNOGRAPHIC MUSEUM

Continue along ul. Augustiańska and turn left into ul. Węgłowa where you will shortly reach **Plac Wolnica**, the former market place of Kazimierz. The square is overlooked by the **Ethnographic Museum** (Muzeum Etnograficzne; Pl. Wolnica 1; tel: 012 430 60 23; entrance on ul. Krakowska 46; Mon 10am–6pm, Wed–Fri 10am–3pm, Sat–Sun 10am–2pm; charge except Sun). This is housed in a splendid early 15th-century building that served as the *ratusz* (town hall) of Kazimierz until 1800 and which was continually extended and restyled until the mid-19th century. The museum was founded in 1947 and features a collection of folk arts and crafts drawn from villages in the regions of Krakow, Podhale and Silesia. These take

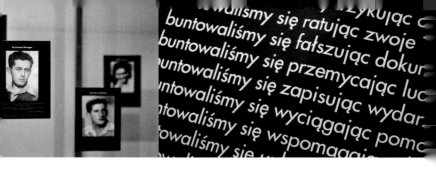

the form of paintings, sculpture and costumes, as well as naive sacral art and Christian exhibits such as Easter eggs painted with rustic motifs. Recreated interiors featuring period furniture are redolent of traditional village homes. The collection extends beyond Poland, with rarities such as late 19th-century Siberian fur coats and folk costumes from Belarus and the Ukraine.

CHURCH OF CORPUS CHRISTI

Leave the square by the northeastern corner, where you will come across the **Church of Corpus Christi ❽** (Kościół Bożego Ciała) on ul. Bożego Ciała. It is another of Krakow's beautiful Gothic churches founded by Casimir the Great. The reason behind the establishment of the church at this particular location is interesting: apparently it was here that fleeing thieves abandoned a monstrance containing the Eucharistic host, which they had stolen from the Kościół Wszystkich Świętych (All Saints' Church), a prominent feature in central Krakow until the 19th century.

Building began in 1340, but the church wasn't completed until the start of the 15th century, when it became the parish church for Roman Catholics living in Kazimierz. King Władysław Jagiełło invited the canons of the Lateran Order to supervise the church – their residences can still be seen across the courtyard by the entrance. Among the Gothic, Renaissance and Baroque elements of this ornate but dignified church is the Renaissance tombstone

of Bartolomeo Bereccio, who designed Sigismund's Chapel and the Gothic stained-glass windows in Wawel Cathedral. The gilded main altar includes a painting of the Nativity by Tommaso Dolabella, while the ornamental pulpit takes the form of a boat.

GALICIA JEWISH MUSEUM

Continue east along ul. św Wawrzynca, turning left into ul. Dajwór, where the **Galicia Jewish Museum ❾** is located at no. 18 (tel: 012 421 68 42; daily May–Oct 9am–7pm; Nov–Apr 9.30am–5.30pm; charge). This photographic exhibition covers Jewish life in Polish Galicia, and the centre additionally hosts Yiddish and Hebrew language courses, concerts and more.

NEW JEWISH CEMETERY

At the end of ul. Dajwór turn right into ul. Miodowa, and walk beyond the viaduct to reach the **New Jewish Cemetery ❿** at no. 55. The cemetery, established at the beginning of the 19th century, contains the graves of many renowned Jews.

Food and Drink 🍴
⑦ **ENZO**
Ul. Bozego Ciała 14; tel: 060 419 51 43; open Sun–Wed noon–midnight, Thur–Sat noon–4am; €€€€
By day a good if flashy café, by night an ultra-trendy hang-out for Krakow's smart set. With space-age design throughout, it is further evidence of Kazimierz's emergence as Krakow's classiest district.

In the Crypt
Local legends Jan Matejko and Stanisław Wyspiański are both buried in the crypt of the Church of Corpus Christi.

NATIONAL MUSEUM

A visit to the National Museum, the city's largest and most comprehensive, and the surrounding area west of the historic centre. For a pleasant picnic lunch, take a detour to Krakow's largest park, Jordan.

DISTANCE 1km (½ mile) not including detour to Jordan Park
TIME A half day
START National Museum
END Capuchin's Church
POINTS TO NOTE

To get to the museum from the Old Town, take tram 15 three stops from Barbican (a short walk north of Main Market Square). To walk directly to the museum from Main Market Square will take around 15 minutes. Note that as you walk in through the main entrance, ahead of you on the ground floor are spaces reserved for temporary exhibitions. Check www.muzeum.krakow.pl for details.

Eating Options
There are few places to eat and drink on this route outside of the hotels listed in the Food and Drink box.

If you want to enjoy a picnic in Jordan Park, it is best to come equipped with food from the city centre (buying groceries at Cloth Hall is always a thrill), as there are few shops in the area of the park itself.

Revered Exhibit
Don't miss the uniform of Józef Piłsudski on the ground floor of the National Museum: Poles look on it with almost religious reverence for its association with the victorious Polish forces of World War I.

NATIONAL MUSEUM

Don't be discouraged by the unattractive, 1930s Modernist architecture of the **National Museum** ❶ (Muzeum Narodowe; al 3 Maja 1; tel: 012 295 55 00; www.muzeum.krakow.pl; May–Oct Tue, Thur 10am–4pm, Wed, Fri, Sat 10am–7pm, Sun 10am–3pm; Nov–Apr Tue, Thur, Sun 10am–3pm, Wed, Fri, Sat 10am–6pm; charge except Thur). This is one of the highlights of the city, and inside is a fabulous array of historic works of art.

Arms and Uniforms Gallery

To the right as you enter the building, this gallery displays an extensive collection of military exhibits, ranging from the Middle Ages to the 20th century,

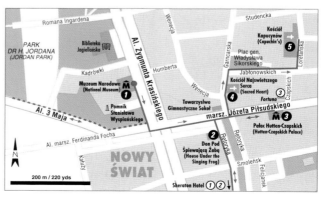

including poignant memorabilia of the 18th- and 19th-century rebellions against partition. The World War II collection features military decorations and medals.

Gallery of Decorative Arts

Covering the Middle Ages to the 20th century, the arts and crafts on the first floor detail Krakow's history as the country's centre of fine art. Here you'll find silver and gold items, sacral art, clocks, glass, and a collection of ceramics that spans Polish and European decorative tiles, faience and porcelain, with examples by Meissen and Sèvres. Polish furniture, particularly from Gdańsk, is well represented in a series of rooms that highlights such genres as Biedermeier, Empire and Secessionist.

20th-Century Polish Art and Sculpture Gallery

More than 600 exhibits on the second floor extend from the Młoda Polska (Young Poland) movement that pioneered Secessionism (Stanisław Wyspiański, Wojciech Weiss, Józef Mehoffer) through the avant-garde Krakow Group of the early 20th century, to modern and contemporary art by the likes of the Expressionist Stanisław Witkiewicz.

JORDAN PARK

A pleasant detour from the route can be made by exiting the museum through the main entrance, turning right along al. Krasińskiego, right again along al. Focha and then bearing right along al. 3 Maja: in a couple of minutes you arrive at the large **Jordan Park** (Park dr H. Jordana), named after a renowned 19th-century Cracovian doctor, and the vast **Błonia** meadow. It's one of the few green spots in the city where picnicking is tolerated, and Jordan will be popular with kids, who can take a paddle boat ride around the artificial lake. There are also plenty of play areas. Football supporters might want to take a look at the stadium of Wisła, Krakow's leading team, at the western end of the park.

MARSZAŁA PIŁSUDSKIEGO STREET

From the entrance of the National Museum, take a right (passing the Wyspiański monument), and then turn left at the main crossroads on to **ul. Marszała Józefa Piłsudskiego** (named after the statesman and inter-war army commander). The main street of the Nowy Świat (New World) district, it is home to some elegant architecture, much of which dates from the early 19th century. You'll find Towarzystwo Gimnastyczne 'Sokół' at no. 27, the gymnasium of an organisation founded in 1867 to promote physical fitness. This was actually a cover for the military training of Krakow's youth during the period of partitions. Opened in 1889, it's the city's oldest gym. Whereas the late 19th-century façade features neo-Gothic elements, the ornamental friezes incorporate graffiti decorations.

On the corner of ul. Piłsudskiego and ul. Retoryka is the **House Under the**

Above from far left: the stark exterior of the National Museum; a gallery within; *Nothing Inside!* by Jadgwiga Sawicka; morning mist in Jordan Park.

Below: details from *Vita Somnium Breve* (Life is but a Brief Dream) by Józef Mehoffer.

Above from left:
exterior detail from
the Capuchin's
Church; House Under
the Singing Frog; St
Anna's Church
outside and inside.

Singing Frog ❷ (Dom Pod Śpiewającą
Żabą). Designed by Teodor Talowski,
it is a prime example of the neighbourhood's 'historic revival' architecture.
Neighbouring buildings at ul. Piłsudskiego 30, 32, 34 and 36 are eclectic
Secessionism. Turning into ul. Retoryka,
numbers 3, 7 and 9 are Talowski cre-
ations from 1887–91. Avoid even
looking at the bland modern blocks on
the other side of the road. For a break
at this stage, take a detour to the end
of ul. Retoryka, to **Someplace Else** and
The Olive in the Sheraton (ul. Powiśle; *see p.114*), see ⑪① and ⑪②.

Hutten-Czapskich Palace

Further along ul. Piłsudskiego at no. 12
is the late 19th-century neo-Renais-

sance **Hutten-Czapskich Palace ❸**
(Pałac Hutten-Czapskich; tel: 012 292
64 40; admission for research by prior
arrangement only), bequeathed by the
Hutten-Czapski family to the National
Museum in 1902. It houses a fine collection of historic coins and notes.

At no. 16 is the attractive neoclassical building where the novelist
Henryk Sienkiewicz, who won the
Nobel Prize for Literature in 1905,
often stayed. Cross the road and you
can stop for a coffee in the **Hotel For-
tuna** (entrance in ul. Czapskich 5; *see
p.116*), see ⑪③.

TWO CHURCHES

Head back west along ul. Piłsudskiego,
and turn right into ul. Garncarska
where the **Church of the Sacred
Heart ❹** (Kościół Najświętszego
Serca) at no. 26 presents a typical combination of a neo-Gothic façade with
a bas-relief of the Madonna and Child
and neoRenaissance and Secessionist
interiors. The church is the centre of
the cult of St Józef Sebastian Pelczar,
a distinguished 19th-century Krakow
University theologian. Pope John Paul
II prayed beside the tomb when he
visited the church in 1991.

Capuchin's Church

Turn right into ul. Jabłonowskich, then
left into ul. Loretańska. **Capuchin's
Church ❺** (Kościół Kapucynów) at no.
11 was commissioned by the Capuchin
Order late in the 17th century in accordance with its vow of poverty – hence its
particularly pronounced air of modesty.

Food and Drink

① SOMEPLACE ELSE
Ul. Powiśle 7 (Sheraton Krakow); tel: 012 662 10 00; Tue–Thur
noon–midnight, Mon, Sun noon–11pm, Fri, Sat noon–1am; €€€
Known to the expat crowd that calls this place home as 'SPE',
this is much more than a hotel restaurant. Americans especially
love the food – a mix of upmarket burgers and Tex Mex – and
live sports. Also a great place to bring the kids.

② THE OLIVE
Ul. Powiśle 7 (Sheraton Krakow); tel: 012 662 10 00; daily
7–10.30am, noon–3.30pm, 6–10.30pm; €€€€
The Sheraton's classier dining option is a sublime mix of
modern service and décor and traditional Mediterranean food.
How they manage to get fish and seafood this fresh so far from
the sea is anyone's guess, but it explains the high prices.

③ HOTEL FORTUNA
Ul. Czapskich 5; tel: 012 422 31 43; daily 9am–1am; €€€
Decent café inside a once great but now slightly faded hotel.
The café retains a real charm, however, a reminder of when
taking coffee was for the privileged only. There are snacks and
cakes on offer, too, and there is a restaurant, which while
serving decent international dishes is perhaps a little overpriced.

HISTORIC COLLEGES & IMPOSING CHURCHES

Visit some of the Jagiellonian University's historic colleges, including Collegium Maius and Collegium Nowodworskiego, and two of the city's most imposing churches, the Franciscan and the Dominican.

ST ANNA'S CHURCH

For a truly flamboyant example of Baroque style, begin at **St Anna's Church ❶** (Kościół św Anny; ul. św Anny 11; daily 9am–noon, 4–7pm). Modelled loosely on Rome's Church of St Andrew della Valle by Tylman of Gameren, who designed many of Poland's most beautiful Baroque structures, St Anna's was built as the university church between 1689 and 1703. The earliest reference to a church on this site dates from 1381.

DISTANCE 1km (½ mile)
TIME A (long) half day
START St Anna's Church
END Main Market Square
POINTS TO NOTE

St Anna's Church is easy to reach from the Main Market Square: walk 250m/yds along ul. Szewska, then take a left turn through the small park. Note that Collegium Maius' museum can only be visited as part of a guided tour; advance booking is recommended.

Dome of St Anna's
The dome of St Anna's Church was painted by Italians Carlo and Innocente Monti and represents the ultimate victory of Catholicism, depicted as Christianity's one true faith.

Above from left:
Collegium Maius:
door detail, assembly
hall and library.

Chopin's Piano
A piano once the
property of Fryderyk
Chopin, the legendary
Polish pianist and
composer, can be
seen in the Green
Hall of the Collegium
Maius. It is part of an
exhibition of national
treasures. Chopin
in fact never
visited Krakow.

After that was destroyed by a fire in 1407, its successor was a Gothic church funded by King Władysław Jagiełło. Extended in 1428, it gained collegiate status in 1535, but was demolished in 1689, having become too small for the congregation. This was partly due to the growing cult of St Jan Kanty, whose tomb is to the right of the main altar. A theology professor at the Jagiellonian University, Kanty was canonised in 1775.

Majestic Frescoes

The degree of ornamentation throughout the church is intense but always ethereally light, with majestic frescoes, particularly in the cupola. Sculptures (including one of St Anna herself) and magnificent stucco designs featuring fruit and floral motifs are the work of the Italian Baltazar Fontana. The 17th-century painting of St Anna on the main altar is by King Jan III Sobieski's court painter, Jerzy Siemiginowski.

COLLEGIUM NOWODWORSKIEGO

Across the road is **Collegium Nowodworskiego** ➋ (Nowodworski College; ul. św Anny 12), which was founded as a grammar school in 1586 by Bartłomiej Nowodworski, one of the king's private secretaries. The present building, the university's Collegium Medicum, complete with arcaded courtyard, dates from 1643 and is the oldest Polish college still in use. The actual building isn't open to the public, but there is permanent access from the street to the courtyard. For those feeling peckish the super **Chimera Salad Bar** is a 50m/yds detour from here further along ul. św Anny at no. 3, see ⑪①. A more substantial feed can be had at **Trattoria Soprano**, see ⑪②.

COLLEGIUM MAIUS

Pick up the walk on ul. Jagiellońska. Now a museum, **Collegium Maius** ➌ (Great College; tel: 012 422 05 49; Mon–Fri 10am–3pm, May–Oct Thur until 6pm, Sat 10am–2pm; charge except Sat) at no. 15 was Poland's first university college (and the second in Central and Eastern Europe after Prague). Entrance to the courtyard is free whenever the college is open (there's a good souvenir shop just off the courtyard), but admission to the museum is only as part of a guided tour (buy tickets from the ground-floor office in the courtyard).

This college originated in Wawel Castle in 1364. In 1400 King Włady-

---

Food and Drink

① SALAD BAR CHIMERA

Ul. św. Anny 3; tel: 012 423 21 78; daily noon–11pm; €€
This salad bar is situated beneath the more formal U Chimera restaurant and comprises several interlinked, high-ceilinged, brick-and-stone-vaulted cellar rooms. Everything tastes fresh, and is served in a friendly manner at the counter. Choose from the likes of herring salad, stuffed tomatoes and various quiches.

② TRATTORIA SOPRANO

Ul. św. Anny 7; tel: 012 422 51 95; daily 10am–11.30pm; €€
Krakow is full of sub-standard Italian restaurants; this is one of the exceptions. You will find good, simple Italian food, such as the spaghetti aglio, olio e peperoncino, at cheap prices. The setting is pleasant: a surprisingly spacious dining room decorated in warm Mediterranean shades.

sław Jagiełło purchased a house on what is now Jagiellońska Street from a wealthy merchant family called Pęcherz to serve as the seat of the college, then known as Academia Cracoviensis. The house was soon extended, and neighbouring houses were acquired and linked by annexes. These buildings burnt down in the late 15th century, and a purpose-built college with an elegant Gothic façade took their place. Completed in 1492, when it became known as Collegium Maius, it included the stunning arcaded cloister, from which 'professors' staircases' lead up to the professorial chambers on the first and second floors. It was refurbished in a neo-Gothic style during the 19th century, with the original Gothic appearance restored between 1949 and 1964.

Professors' Dining Room

The professors' common room, the treasury, assembly hall and library were built in 1507–19 in Gothic style. The library features a beautifully painted skyscape on the vaulted ceiling, as well as historic portraits and various rare tomes – it became the university library in 1860. The former professors' dining room has distinctive Gdańsk cupboards and an extensive collection of gold and silver tableware.

Copernicus Room

The **Mikołaj Kopernik Room** commemorates the life of the renowned astronomer Nicholas Copernicus, who studied here in 1491–5. His then rev-

olutionary theory that the sun and not the earth was the centre of the universe, and that the earth and planets revolved around the sun, was set forth in *De Revolutionibus Orbium Coelestium*, which he completed in 1530 after studying in Bologna, Padua and Rome.

His work provided a foundation for subsequent theories by astronomers such as Galileo. Handwritten sections of the original manuscript can be seen in the Copernicus Room, together with a collection of historic portraits, astrolabes (navigational aids that measure the altitude of stars and the planets) and other astronomical instruments from the 1480s. A 1510 golden globe, one of the first to show the New World, bears the inscription *America, terra noviter reperta* (America, a newly discovered land). The walls of the *aula* (assembly hall) feature more than 100 paintings, including portraits of King Władysław Jagiełło and his wife Queen Jadwiga.

Collegium Maius Tickets
In summer it's advisable to reserve your tickets for the Collegium Maius in advance, either at the museum office, or by phone.

Below: astrolabe in the Copernicus Room.

Nicholas Copernicus

Polish astronomer Nicholas Copernicus (1473–1543) was the first person to formulate a scientifically based heliocentric cosmology that displaced the earth from the centre of the universe. Born in Toruń in central Poland to wealthy parents, Copernicus was by profession an economist, mathematician and diplomat, often carrying out delicate business for the Polish King Sigismund I. Astronomy was for Copernicus very much a hobby pursued only when time allowed, making his achievements all the more incredible. It was his work above anything else that made the Jagiellonian University one of the most respected seats of learning in the whole of Renaissance Europe. (For Matejko's portrait *see p.69*.)

Bishops of Krakow
There are portraits of Krakow's bishops from the 15th century onwards hanging in the cloister of the Basilica of St Francis.

BASILICA OF ST FRANCIS

Turn left into ul. Gołębia, where if you fancy a good, relaxing coffee you can head into the bizarrely named **Migrena** (migraine) café, see ③. Then take a right into ul. Bracka, leading to the **Basilica of St Francis of Assisi ❹** (Bazylika św Franciszka z Asyżu; entrance from ul. Franciszkańska 1, or Plac Wszystkich Świętych 5; daily 9am–3pm). Striking in its imposing beauty, this church was founded for the Franciscan Order, which arrived in Krakow in 1237 at the invitation of Duke Henryk Pobożny (Henry the Devout). Designed in the form of a Greek cross, and built in a Gothic style between 1252

Below: cloisters at the Dominican Church.

and 1269, it was greatly extended during the 15th century thanks to King Bolesław Wstydliwy (Boleslaus the Bashful), who is buried here.

Tadeusz Popiel Mosaic
The Great Fire of Krakow in 1850 destroyed some historic features and resulted in further rebuilding in a neo-Gothic style. But the church has retained historic elements, such as the Gothic galleries and fragments of wall paintings in the adjoining Franciscan monastery. By the Baroque altar, the apse features a Tadeusz Popiel mosaic depicting St Francis of Assisi. The Chapel of Our Lady the Sorrowful, itself the size of a small church, has a

Food and Drink

③ **MIGRENA**
Ul. Gołębia 3; tel: 012 430 24 18; Mon–Sat 9am–11pm, Sun 10am–11pm; €€
Wonderful café where a Far Eastern, Buddhist-style atmosphere (complete with mellow, Zen-like music) makes for a wonderful venue to unwind. You can both escape from the crowds here and meet local students, for whom it is something of a legend.

④ **PIERWSZY LOKAL**
Ul. Stolarska 6/1; tel: 012 431 24 41; Mon–Fri 6.30am–midnight, Sat, Sun 10am–1am; €€€€
Opening up early for office workers who take breakfast and coffee here, this place serves as a typical Krakow café during the day before transforming into a hip and trendy bar and late-night venue as the sun goes down. Relatively expensive, but good value for money.

15th-century painting of the Madonna, and fine polychrome.

Mehoffer and Wyspiański

The church showcases the work of two of the country's greatest Secessionist artists. The paintings representing the Stations of the Cross are by Józef Mehoffer, while the stunning polychromy on the walls and vaulted ceilings was designed by Stanisław Wyspiański. The effect of this intense combination of Gothic and floral motifs with Secessionist elements is dazzling, though it can take a little time to appreciate while you adjust your eyes to the church's sombre lighting. Paradoxically, the semi-darkness heightens the beauty of the stained-glass windows, also designed by Wyspiański. For a genuinely spiritual experience, stand in the main nave and look up at the most important of these windows, over the main entrance. The lilac-and-blue palette, completed in 1900, is an astonishing depiction of the Creation *(see pp.8–9)*.

DOMINICAN CHURCH

Another extraordinary ecclesiastical centre is just across the square. The Basilica of the Holy Trinity, commonly known as the **Dominican Church and Monastery** ❺ (Kościół Dominikanów; ul. Stolarska 12; daily 7am–7pm), is as august and austere as the Franciscan church, although the building represents a very different tradition. Its character is immediately indicated by the highly geometric, neo-Gothic façade.

The church originated in 1220, when the Dominicans reached Poland. The first, Romanesque, church, destroyed by the Tartars in 1241, was greatly extended during the 15th century, when Renaissance elements were added.

The **Chapel of St Dominic**, who founded the Order in Italy, is one of the most beautiful examples of Renaissance art in Poland, while the Rococo **Chapel of Our Lady of the Rosary**, which dates from 1685, contains a painting of the Madonna copied from the painting of Our Lady of the Rosary in Rome's Basilica of St Maria Maggiore.

You can also see the cloisters in the adjoining Dominican Monastery, where many of the city's most illustrious residents were laid to rest.

STOLARSKA STREET

Adjoining **ul. Stolarska**, which extends to the edge of the Small Market Place, was named after the carpenters who once plied their trade in workshops here (*stolarz* is Polish for carpenter). A great little café at no. 6, **Pierwszy Lokal**, see ⑪④, serves big pots of steaming tea for tired tourists. A wooden arcade on one side of the street (nos 8–10) features various specialist shops, including a jeweller, an antiquarian bookshop and, displaying graphic art exhibited at the city's foremost art shows, the **Galeria Plakatu** (Poster Gallery). The grand buildings on the other side of the road house the French, German and American consulates.

At the end of ul. Stolarska turn left and head towards Main Market Square.

Above from far left: mosaic at the Basilica of St Francis; the Dominican Church and Monastery; the Madonna in the Chapel of Our Lady of the Rosary.

TWO HISTORIC THOROUGHFARES

Grodzka Street (ul. Grodzka) combines imposing town houses, august institutions and stunning churches; the adjoining Street of the Canons (ul. Kanoniczna), one of the city's most exquisite streets, boasts several museums.

Corpus Christi
Though ul. Grodzka no longer plays host to royal processions, each year on Corpus Christi (Boże Ciało in Polish), a major parade of locals in traditional dress makes its way from Wawel to the Main Market Square.

DISTANCE 1km (½ mile)
TIME A (long) half day
START Ul. Grodzka
END Church of the Missionary Priests
POINTS TO NOTE
Ul. Grodzka was the southern part of the Royal Route, which took kings from Florian's Gate to Wawel. Pick it up at the southeastern corner of Main Market Square. Note that this is a long route and involves walking along often very crowded, narrow streets. There are plenty of good restaurants en route, however, and a good idea is to take an early lunch before heading off.

Food and Drink

① POD ANIOŁAMI
Ul. Grodzka 35; tel: 012 421 39 99; daily 1–10pm; €€€
Pod Aniołami (Under the Angels) is one of Krakow's most popular restaurants. It's located in a large cellar decorated with 'folk chic' touches, and features open cooking ranges. A lovely patio garden at the rear is perfect for alfresco dining. The grilled *oscypek* (smoked ewe's cheese, a speciality of the Tatras) is a highlight.

② MIOD MALINA
Ul. Grodzka 40; tel: 012 430 04 11; daily noon–11pm; €€€
With one of the most welcoming hearths in all Poland, this gorgeous little restaurant is unsurprisingly packed out most evenings, so you'll need to book ahead. The food is good, mainly based around Lesser Poland cuisine, with plenty of game.

Ul. Grodzka is straddled on both sides by the Okół district of the city, believed to be the site of the first Cracovian settlement outside of Wawel. Given the area's fair sprinkling of small parks, it has a much greener feel to it than the rest of the Old Town.

GRODZKA STREET

The long and beautiful **ul. Grodzka** ❶, a major thoroughfare that leads from the Main Market Square to Wawel Castle, comprises a fascinating mixture of restaurants, cafés and bars, shops and galleries. Its origins actually pre-date Krakow's town charter (1257) – it was probably established as a principal street in the 9th century. Ul. Grodzka was traditionally known as Droga Solna (The Salt Road) because it heads off towards the Wieliczka and Bochnia salt mines.

Historic Façades
Among the most attractive houses, **House Under the Lion** (Dom Pod Lwem) at no. 32 has a 14th-century stone lion carved above the portal. **Under the Angels** (Pod Aniołami) at no. 35 is a delightful Polish restaurant and café with an atmospheric vaulted cellar decorated in a folksy style and

with a charming patio garden, see
⑪①. At no. 38, **House Under the
Elephants** (Dom Pod Elefanty) is
thought to have been the residence and
premises of Bonifazio Cantelli, a 17th-
century royal apothecary. The exotic
animals depicted on the façade formed
a typical apothecary's sign – not to be
confused with the golden elephant at
no. 11 Plac Wszystkich Świętych *(see
p.73)*. There is another excellent Polish
restaurant at no. 40, **Miod Malina**, see
⑪②. Across the road, **Wit Stwosz's**
(Veit Stoss') **House** (Dom Wit Stwos-
za) at nos 39–41 was the residence of
the master carver from Nuremberg
from 1478 to 1492.

Turn into ul. Poselska and at no. 21
you'll find the Baroque **St Joseph's
Church ②** (Kosciół św Józefa) and the
adjoining Bernardine Convent.

Back on ul. Grodzka at no. 53 is the
Jagiellonian University's **Collegium
Iuridicum ③**, which dates from the
14th century, and was restyled and
extended in the 16th century. This
college houses the university's history
of art faculty and, beyond an attractive Baroque portal, features an
arcaded courtyard.

Church of St Peter and St Paul

Opposite, the **Church of St Peter and
St Paul ④** (Kościół św Piotra i Pawła;
no. 54) is a transcendent example of
Baroque architecture approached
through a walled courtyard (originally
the church graveyard) set with 12 late
Baroque sculptures of the Apostles
(1720s). The courtyard is a highly aesthetic overture to a magnificent

Baroque façade designed by Zygmunt
III Waza's architect Giovanni Battista
Trevano. Commissioned by the Jesuits,
who came to Krakow in 1583, the
design was modelled on two churches
in Rome, San Andrea della Valle and
Il Gesù, following the form of a Latin
cross. Additional Baroque elements

Above from far left:
House Under the
Elephants; at a café-
bar on ul. Grodzka;
door lantern; the 12
Apostles at the
Church of St Peter
and St Paul.

Below: detail
from a façade on
ul. Grodzka; House
Under the Lion.

The Polish Pope
Karol Wojtyła, later
to become Pope
John Paul II, moved
to Krakow as a
student in 1939, to
study literature at
the Jagellonian
University. His first
home in the city was
at ul. Tyniecka 10,
just across the
Wisła from the
Grunwaldzki bridge.

were also added by Trevano. The impressive stucco work, at its finest in the apse, where it depicts scenes from the lives of St Peter and St Paul (1619–33), is by Giovanni Battista Falconi.

The tomb of Fr Piotr Skarga (1536–1612), Poland's most famous preacher, can be seen in the crypt. People still leave pleas for his intercession next to his tomb.

Church of St Andrew the Apostle

An equally fine architectural paradigm is the neighbouring **Church of St Andrew the Apostle** ❺ (Kościół św Andrzeja Apostoła; no. 56). An early Romanesque church with a pair of elegant towers, it was founded at the end of the 11th century and withstood the Tartar siege of 1241 thanks to 1.5m (5ft) thick walls. The exquisite Baroque interiors are on a far smaller scale than the façade suggests. Wall paintings by Balthazar Fontana and 18th-century stucco work are set

between a vaulted ceiling decorated with putti and acanthus leaves, and a stunning 18th-century marble floor. The highly gilded altar is matched by a gilded limewood pulpit in the form of a fishing boat with putti clinging to the soaring mast. Adjoining the church is the 14th-century Order of St Claire (Klasztor Klarysek), established in Poland in 1245 at the behest of Duke Leszek Biały.

STREET OF THE CANONS

In front of the two churches, a small square named after St Mary Magdalene features a statue of Fr Piotr Skarga (1536–1612), and leads to the tranquil **ul. Kanonicza** (Street of the Canons). This street of ornate houses and palaces was named after the clergymen from Wawel Castle who lived here in the 15th and 16th centuries.

Buildings of Note

At the northern end of the street, no. 1 has an impressive Baroque portal. The **Cricoteka Museum** ❻ (no. 5; tel: 012 422 83 32; Mon–Fri 10am–2pm; charge) is home to the Centre for the Documentation of the Art of Tadeusz Kantor, which traces the rise of the avant-garde Cricot 2 Theatre, and is a good example of Gothic architecture. Contrast this with the Renaissance façade of the **House Under Three Crowns** (Dom Pod Trzema Koronami) at no. 7. Look hard above the plain Renaissance portal of no. 6 to see the dingy wall painting of the Madonna of Częchostowa. Number 9 is a late

---

Food and Drink 🍴

③ DEMMER'S TEA HOUSE
Ul. Kanonicza 21; tel: 012 423 16 60; daily 10am–10pm; €€
Classic cellar tea bar where the star of the show is the famous Demmer tea of Vienna, drunk in these parts for centuries. Staff are hired for their love of tea and will talk you through the many different varieties. The place itself has a small but lively cellar where the rough hewn walls are part of the attraction.

④ U LITERATÓW
Ul. Kanonicza 7; tel: 012 421 86 66; daily 10am–10pm; €€
Still a firm favourite with Krakow's literary set, this café is a reminder of the days when cafés meant coffee, cigarettes and discussion. A cobbled courtyard garden provides alfresco tables, while *fin de siècle* town house interiors with a piano and comfy sofas create a time capsule of charm and elegance.

14th-century mansion (refurbished in the 19th century), while no. 18 is the seat of the John Paul II Institute.

Archdiocesan Museum

The historic building at no. 19 is the **Archdiocesan Museum** ❼ (Muzeum Archidiecezjalne; tel: 012 421 89 63; Tue–Fri 10am–4pm, Sat–Sun 10am–3pm; charge). Its collection includes sacral art – paintings, sculpture, and illuminated manuscripts – from the 12th to the 18th centuries. The Gothic sculptures of the Madonna and Child, and also the altar-pieces, are particularly impressive.

Between 1952 and 1967, when he was Bishop of Krakow, Pope John Paul II used a room in the Archdiocesan Museum as a study. You can visit a replica of his room, which includes a variety of personal effects.

Deacon's House

The **Deacon's House** ❽ (Dom Dziekański) at no. 21 is a gem. Originally late 14th-century, it features a spectacular portal and an arcaded cloister added in the 16th century by Italian architect Santi Gucci. The 14th-century house at no. 25 was once that of the medieval chronicler Jan Długosz, and subsequently the studio of Stanisław Wyspiański's father, a sculptor.

Coffee Among the Literati

A perfect retreat for a tea break is **Demmer's Tea House** at no. 21, which offers a choice of 130 types of tea, see ⑪③. If you prefer coffee try **U Liter-** **atów** (Among the Literati) café at no. 7, see ⑪④.

Church of the Missionary Priests

Return to ul. Grodzka, head south in the direction of the Wawel and you'll find ul. Stradomska, a busy, gritty street with the beautiful **Church of the Missionary Priests** ❾ (Kościół Księży Misjonarzy) at no. 4.

The Church of the Missionary Priests was established in France by St Vincent a Paulo in 1625, who came to Krakow in 1682 to set up a seminary for priests at Wawel Castle. This particular church was completed between 1719 and 1728 in a late Baroque style. The façade was inspired by Bernini's Sant' Andrea al Quirinale Church in Rome, while the stylised interiors were based on Borromini's work in some of Rome's finest churches, such as the Chapel of the Three Kings in the Palazzo di Propaganda Fide and the Gesù and Maria Church.

Above from far left: ul. Kanonicza; the Archdiocesan Museum; façade detail; the exterior of the Church of the Missionary Priests was inspired by Bernini.

Below: tourists on ul. Kanonicza.

MATEJKO SQUARE

Explore the north of the city around Matejko Square (Plac Matejki), a showpiece of late 19th- and early 20th-century styles and home to some of Krakow's most notable historic buildings and ancient churches.

Matejko Square

Plac Matejki is named after Jan Matejko (1838–93), a son of Krakow widely regarded as Poland's finest 19th-century painter. He was able to capture events with searing accuracy and without the need for allegory, and many of his works are viewed as historical documents.

DISTANCE 1km (½ mile)

TIME A half day

START Matejko Square

END Church of the Nuns of the Visitation

POINTS TO NOTE

Leave the historic centre along ul. Floriańska, proceed through Florian's Gate and continue past the Barbican.

Food and Drink

① JAREMA

Pl. Matejki 5; tel: 012 429 36 69; daily noon–11pm; €€€

Behind a charming façade, Eastern Polish cuisine dominates the menu here, including dishes from Lithuania, (once, of course, a Polish province).

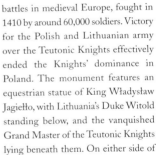

MATEJKO SQUARE

The central feature of **Plac Matejki** is the **Monument to the Battle of Grunwald ①** (Pomnik Grunwaldzki). This commemorates one of the greatest battles in medieval Europe, fought in 1410 by around 60,000 soldiers. Victory for the Polish and Lithuanian army over the Teutonic Knights effectively ended the Knights' dominance in Poland. The monument features an equestrian statue of King Władysław Jagiełło, with Lithuania's Duke Witold standing below, and the vanquished Grand Master of the Teutonic Knights lying beneath them. On either side of the monument victorious Polish knights collect Teutonic flags. Opposite is the Polish restaurant **Jarema**, see ⑪①.

Academy of Fine Arts

The square's architecture is eclectic. Its largest building is the monumental and opulent **Polish State Railways Headquarters** at no. 12 (closed to the public). Combining neoclassicism and neo-Baroque, it is nakedly Viennese in both size and style. Next to it at no. 13, the **Academy of Fine Arts** (Akademia Sztuk Pięknych; tel: 012 299 20 13; open by prior appointment only) has a façade designed in 1879 by Maciej Moraczewski featuring a bust

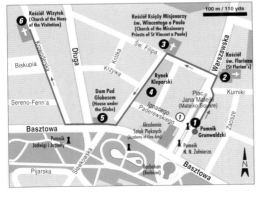

of Poland's finest painter, Jan Matejko, above the main entrance. Matejko was instrumental in establishing the academy before becoming its first rector.

St Florian's Church

In the northeastern corner of the square is **St Florian's Church ❷** (Kościół św Floriana). The church was built to house the remains of St Florian, which were brought to Poland in 1184 at the instigation of King Kazimierz Sprawiedliwy (Casimir the Righteous). St Florian, who became one of Krakow's patron saints, is shown in a 1686 painting near the main altar, and in cartouches depicting scenes from his life.

Consecrated in 1212, the church was originally built in a Romanesque style that was lost in refurbishments. Extensive early 20th-century restorations yielded the current blend of Gothic, Italianate Baroque and Rococo. Admire a 15th-century bas-relief of the Virgin Mary and a 1767 chapel dedicated to St Jan Kanty.

AROUND THE SQUARE

Leave St Florian's and head west along św Filipa. On your right at no. 19 is the **Church of the Missionary Priests of St Vincent a Paolo ❸** (Kościół Księży Misjonarzy św Wincentego a Paulo), a centre for the cult of Our Lady of Lourdes. Built in 1876–7, it was extended (in 1911–12) to include a chapel with an emotive figure of Our Lady of Lourdes. This statue and a painting of the Crucifixion are both said to have miraculous powers.

House Under the Globe

Head south past the brick stalls of **Kleparz Market ❹** (Rynek Kleparski; daily 7am–6pm), and turn right into ul. Basztowa: ahead of you is the 1906 **House Under the Globe ❺** (Dom Pod Globusem) at the junction with ul. Długa. This, a geometric and uniform example of Secessionism, has none of the sense of colour and flamboyance evident in the city's other buildings of this period. Designed, and still used, as commercial premises, the building has a distinctive spire, with gargoyles in the form of eagles, topped by a globe.

Church of the Nuns of the Visitation

Continue along ul. Basztowa, turn right into ul. Krowoderska and you'll find the **Church of the Nuns of the Visitation ❻** (Kościół Wizytek) at no. 16. The church is under the patronage of St Francis Salesian, whose mission was to provide religious education for the young. Designed by Giovanni Solari and the Jesuit priest and architect Stanisław Solski, it was consecrated in 1695. This exquisite Baroque building has a magnificent façade featuring an abundance of statuary. The stylised interiors include more statuary, especially by the main altar, beautiful side chapels, magnificent 17th-century polychrome and ornate stucco work. Also said to have miraculous powers is a painting of *Matki Boskiej Nieustającej Pomocy* (Our Lady of Eternal Intercession), originally from Rome. The Nuns of the Visitation convent, built around an attractive garden, adjoins the church.

Above from far left: Monument to the Battle of Grunwald; House Under the Globe; street scene.

Polish Grub

For good, cheap Polish food served in huge portions by warm, friendly staff, you can't do much better than Diabelska Kuchni restaurant in Kleparz Market. The place itself is a riot of local earthenware and folk art (Rynek Kleparski 14; tel: 012 422 35 92; Mon–Sat 10am–9pm, Sun 11am–9pm).

Below: Church of the Nuns of the Visitation.

CHURCHES OF EASTERN KRAKOW

Simply by strolling along ul. Mikołaja Kopernika (Nicholas Copernicus Street) you can see an astonishing number of sensational and historic churches; en route you can take a break at the Botanical Garden.

DISTANCE 1.5km (1 mile)
TIME A half day
START St Nicholas' Church
END Celestat Museum
POINTS TO NOTE
From Main Market Square walk east towards the Westerplatte to pick up ul. Mikołaja Kopernika. Tram nos 9, 10, 13 and 14 all run along the Westerplatte and stop at the junction with ul. Kopernika. Eat before setting off and bring something to drink with you, as there are no restaurants and bars en route. Bear in mind, too, that the Botanical Garden is closed during the winter.

Densely lined with leafy trees, ul. Mikołaja Kopernika is a majestic promenade. Lined with stately homes, well-kept gardens and quiet court-yards, it was once home to the city's richest people, and today hosts some of its most revered academic institutions.

ST NICHOLAS' CHURCH

The city's oldest church is **St Nicholas' Church ❶** (Kościół św Mikołaja; open during services only) at no. 9. The earliest reference to this church dates from the 12th century, before it was rebuilt in a Romanesque style in 1229. In 1467 it was taken over by the Benedictine Order – which had been

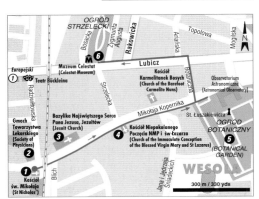

established at the Abbey of Tyniec just outside Krakow since the 11th century. For all the Gothic restyling of the 15th century, and the addition of Baroque elements between 1677 and 1684, a fair number of original Romanesque sections have survived. Admire the main altar, which features a painting of St Nicholas, and also the baptismal font and a pentaptych of the Coronation of the Blessed Virgin Mary, which are both Gothic. The courtyard's medieval sculpture, known as the 'Lamp of the Dead', resembles a miniature church tower.

SOCIETY OF PHYSICIANS

Opposite the church, on the left-hand side of ul. Radziłłowska, take a look at the **Society of Physicians** ❷ (Gmach Towarzystwa Lekarskiego; no. 14; daily 10am–3pm; free). It was built in 1904 and made sublime by its interiors, many designed by Stanisław Wyspiański. Its stained-glass window featuring Apollo is one of Krakow's hidden treasures.

JESUIT CHURCH

Back on ul. Kopernika, head past the railway bridge and look to your left. The **Jesuit Church** ❸ (Bazylika Najświętszego Serca Pana Jezusa, Jezuitów; daily 9am–noon and during services) at no. 26 is an extraordinary example of *fin de siècle* Modernism, not just in terms of style, but also in scale – it's 52m (170ft) long, 19m (62ft) wide and has a 68m (223ft) high tower. First established in 1868, it evolved from a much smaller chapel attached to a Jesuit college for

novices. In 1893 the Jesuits decided to turn the chapel into a church that would be Poland's centre of the cult of the Sacred Heart. It was designed by the celebrated architect Franciszek Mączyński and completed in 1912.

A number of the country's finest artists and craftsmen were commissioned to work on the church. Note the entrance portal and integral sculptures by Ksawery Dunikowski. Particularly dazzling are Brother Wojciech Pieczowka's series of mosaics, and the magnificent *Hołd Narodu Polskiego Sercu Bożemu* (Homage of the Polish Nation to the Sacred Heart) designed by Piotr Stachiewicz and imported from Venice.

The Bukowski Murals

Amazingly vivid Secessionist murals with floral motifs by Jan Bukowski extend along a nave that's remarkable for its granite and marble pillars. The neo-Renaissance main altar, with a colonnade supporting statuary, and a mosaic extending along the apse, is highly unusual and deeply emotive. A more recent addition is the Chapel of the Eternal Adoration of the Blessed Sacrament, completed in 1960, when the church was classified as a basilica.

CHURCH OF THE IMMACULATE CONCEPTION

Continue along ul. Kopernika; hospital buildings line both sides of the road. On the right at no. 19, set behind a walled forecourt, is the mid-17th-century Baroque **Church of the Immaculate**

Carmelite Church

At ul. Kopernika 44 is the Church of the Barefoot Carmelite Nuns (open only during services), a small convent church worth seeing for its oversized entrance, complete with Corinthian columns and elegant Baroque motifs.

Below: the tranquil Botanical Garden.

Conception of the Blessed Virgin Mary and St Lazarus ❹ (Kosciół Niepokolanego Poczęcia NMP i św Łazarza; daily 8am–4pm). Since the 18th century, this has been the official church of the city's main hospital. Its most fascinating feature is a remarkable vaulted ceiling, painted a vivid blue.

BOTANICAL GARDEN

At the end of the street, on the right, is the **Botanical Garden** ❺ (Ogród Botaniczny; tel: 012 663 36 35; www.ogrod. uj.edu.pl; daily Apr–Oct 9am–7pm, greenhouses Sat–Thur 10am–6pm; charge), which, established in 1783, is Poland's oldest such reserve. Originally comprising a mere 2.5ha (6 acres), it was laid out as an English-style landscaped park in 1820. Some of the trees planted then can be seen in the arboretum. The gardens were extended to their current size of almost 10ha (25 acres) after World War II, and in the 1960s lots of

tropical specimens were added, with extra greenhouses to house them.

The Garden

The garden is an adjunct of the university, and it has always emphasised its educational aspect. Any number of botanists have learnt about their subject here, and the grounds are punctuated by statues of the country's leading figures in the field. In addition to the arboretum, there are medicinal shrubs, Alpine plants (including specimens from the Carpathian Mountains, the Balkans, the Caucasus and the Alps), ponds, pools and lawns with ornamental borders. Two palm houses feature tropical and subtropical plants.

Museum

A small **museum** (Apr–Oct Wed, Fri 10am–2pm, Sat 11am–3pm) housed in an attractive *fin de siècle* villa comprises a couple of galleries, though most exhibits are labelled only in

Polish. Among the exhibits are plant specimens and old prints and maps that outline the Garden's origins and evolution. One of the most interesting exhibits is a display cabinet inlaid with 260 types of wood, culled from trees native to or cultivated in Poland.

MARKSMENS' FRATERNITY

From the Botanical Garden head north along ul. Botaniczna and turn left into ul. Lubicz. About 300m/yds along is the **Celestat Museum** ❻ (Muzeum Celestat; ul. Lubicz 16; tel: 012 429 37 91; Tue–Wed, Fri–Sat 9am–4pm, Thur 11am–6pm; charge), situated on the right within a park. This unusual museum recounts the history of an organisation that has been an integral element of the city for centuries. Still extant, the Bractwo Kurkowe (literally 'Marksmen's Fraternity') was established in medieval times to teach Krakow's civilians how to wield a rifle, should they be needed to defend the city.

The museum's collection includes portraits of champion marksmen and, of course, the club's mascot, the Silver Cockerel, which is a magnificent example of Renaissance art.

The brotherhood's Corpus Christi procession, with participants dressed in historic uniforms, is an annual highlight in the Old Town. Three weeks later, in a traditional ceremony on the Main Market Square, the outgoing king of the brotherhood ceremonially presents the Silver Cockerel to the new incumbent. A short distance from the museum the Ogród Strzelecki (Rifle Marksmen's Garden) is home to monuments to two Polish kings: Jan III Sobieski (1675–96) and Zygmunt August (1548–73), as well as to Pope John Paul II (1920–2005).

Probably famished, walk a little further along Lubicz, under the railway bridge and past the Teatr Buckleina (Buckleina Theatre), to the **Europejski Hotel**, whose **Kossakowka** restaurant serves decent Polish food, see ⑪①.

Continue west on ul. Lubicz to reach the northeastern corner of the Planty.

Sarmatism

Sarmatism was the predominant lifestyle and culture of the Polish *szlachta*, or nobility, from the 16th to the 19th century. It was based on the almost certainly fictitious belief that the Poles are the descendants of the Sarmatians, a group of people who lived north of the Black Sea from the 6th century BC to around the 3rd century AD. Polish Sarmatian culture evolved during the Renaissance from a movement of honourable pacifists into a full-blown warrior culture, which valued horse-riding skills and lavish oriental clothing (not to mention vast handlebar moustaches). Sarmatism faded away from the middle of the 18th century, but a pale shadow of it lives on in modern-day Krakow in the form of the Markmen's Fraternity.

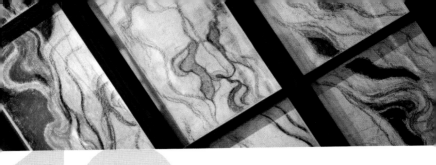

MUSEUMS & GALLERIES

A look at some of Krakow's more specialised museums and galleries, including the preserved homes of Jan Matejko and Józef Mehoffer, modern art centres, the Pharmacy Museum and the Wyspiański Museum.

DISTANCE 1.5km (1 mile)
TIME A full day
START Jan Matejko Museum
END Józef Mehoffer House
POINTS TO NOTE

Pick up this route halfway along ul. Floriańska, a short walk from either Main Market Square or Florian's Gate. The time it takes to complete will depend greatly on how much time is spent in each museum: to do each museum properly a full day will be required, though by speed-viewing the museums a half day will prove to be sufficient. Note that most museums mentioned are closed Mondays.

Food and Drink

① JAMA MICHALIKA

Ul. Floriańska 45; tel: 012 422 15 61; Sun–Thur 9am–10pm, Fri–Sat 9am–11pm; €€

Open for more than a century, this café was one of the primary meeting places of the Młoda Polska (Young Poland) art movement. Almost all of the décor is original, from the stained-glass windows to the artworks that adorn the walls. Expensive coffee and cakes are served by staff who can sometimes let this otherwise sublime place down with their surliness.

The Busiest Street

For much of the 19th century ul. Floriańska was the city's busiest street. Now closed to all but very limited traffic, it was the first street in Krakow to get a tram-line (1881) which ran from the railway station to Main Market Square.

By any standards, Krakow is well served by museums. These range from the vast National Museum *(see pp.50–1)* to a series of fascinating mini-museums designed to document specific themes, historical eras and celebrated artists.

JAN MATEJKO MUSEUM

After taking a coffee at the historic **Jama Michalika** café at ul. Floriańska 45, see ⑪①, make your way two doors down to the **Jan Matejko Museum** ❶ (Dom Jana Matejki; tel: 012 422 59 26; May–Oct: Tue, Wed, Sat 10am–7pm, Thur–Fri 10am–4pm, Sun 10am–3pm; Nov–Apr: Wed–Thur, Sat–Sun 10am–3.30pm, Fri 10am–6pm; charge except Thur). First opened to the public in 1896, this is Poland's oldest biographical museum. Generally considered the greatest artist in the country's history, Matejko (1838–93) spent most of his life in this house, which comprehensively details his body of work, including portraits, sculpture and his designs for the polychromy, stained-glass windows and altarpieces of some of Krakow's finest churches. Matejko's oeuvre has a resonance that goes far beyond his considerable influence on his contemporaries. At a time when Poland was partitioned and therefore didn't offi-

cially exist, his works were exhibited throughout Europe, and thus became an important symbol of Polish identity.

Matejko's Home

The museum has preserved the atmosphere of a private home, with the earliest sections dating from the 15th century. The grand first-floor salon overlooking ul. Floriańska is furnished exactly as it was when Matejko lived here. There's neo-Renaissance furniture commissioned by the artist in Venice in 1878, a cabinet displaying some of his many awards and, in his bedroom, a beautifully painted skyscape ceiling. Self-portraits illustrate the young Matejko; a terracotta bust depicts him as an elderly maestro. Two galleries overlooking the inner courtyard show Matejko's designs for polychromy in St Mary's on Main Market Square.

Matejko's Mementoes

Matejko's keen eye for period detail is also reflected in his collection of antique military and architectural pieces, a number of which can be found in the museum.

You can also see a wooden horse complete with a ceremonial saddle on which his subjects could pose, and other mementoes such as Matejko's palette, spectacles, chess set and walking stick.

Above from far left: a design for Wyspiański's stained-glass window in the Basilica of St Francis *(see p.56)* at the museum dedicated to his work *(see p.71)*; bust of Jan Matejko on the Palace of Art on Plac Szczepański *(see p.72).*

Left: *Nicholas Copernicus by Jan Matejko.*

MUSEUM OF PHARMACY

For a thorough account of the history of the pharmacy, pay a visit to the **Museum of Pharmacy** ❷ (Muzeum Farmacji; tel: 012 421 92 79; Tue noon–6pm, Wed–Sat 10am–2.30pm, closed Sun; charge) also on ul. Floriańska, at no. 25. The museum occupies an elegant town house with a Renaissance portal, as well as Gothic and Baroque elements, and doesn't limit itself to its ostensible subject; it also covers interiors and decorative arts.

The highlights of the various galleries are the replicated interiors of pharmacies throughout history. Also be sure to check out a fascinating collection of assorted urns, jars and other pharmaceutical accessories.

Cellars

In the museum's cellars you will find antique distillation equipment and wine barrels. There was a time when, in the belief that alcohol promoted longevity and youthfulness, Polish apothecaries sold Italian and Hungarian wines – and, this being Poland, vodka – for medicinal purposes. Red wine was thought to be particularly beneficial.

First Floor

The beautiful 19th-century stained-glass window on the first floor landing that pictures a pestle, mortar and various herbs was taken from a chemist's shop in the city. The portrait gallery depicts various renowned apothecaries, while the reconstructed interiors show how pharmacies were furnished in various architectural styles. These include superb 19th-century neo-Baroque and Biedermeier examples. A stunning collection of porcelain and glass urns, used to store various ingredients, are complemented by calligraphically handwritten prescriptions. Exhibits of related items feature a collection of stamps from around the world that have pharmaceutical themes.

Food and Drink

② AMARONE
Pod Różą Hotel, ul. Floriańska 14; tel: 012 424 33 81; daily noon–11pm; €€€€€
Amarone's large atrium-style dining room blends the trappings of modernity with some carefully placed Etruscan (pre-Roman) details, while a few separate dining rooms offer an excellent 'Roman villa'-style eating experience. If you're happy to stick with standard Italian fare, there's a good range of dishes. A great start is being served an *amuse-gueule* (a mini pre-starter that, in Krakow, is a real innovation), followed by a main course of *pappardelle* (ribboned macaroni) with wild mushrooms, and a dessert of almonds in chocolate sauce. An extensive Italian wine list is another bonus. Elegantly dressed tables attract a suitably dressed-up crowd.

③ CHERUBINO
Ul. św Tomasza 15; tel: 012 429 40 07; Mon–Sat noon–midnight, Sun noon–11pm; €€€
A Tuscan/Polish menu includes delicious favourites from each cuisine: antipasti, minestrone, risotto, *pierogi*. One dining room contains 18th- and 19th-century carriages and an ornate tiled stove, the other is rustic-chic Tuscan, with a wood-fired oven and a beamed ceiling.

④ MORSKIE OKO
Pl. Szczepański 8; tel: 012 431 24 23; daily noon–11pm; €€€€
This restaurant has tried to save people the trouble of going to Zakopone by bringing the mountains to the people. Expect plenty of game, mountain stews and rich broths accompanied with lashings of smoked pork fat. Add in the hunting prizes that adorn the walls and you have an enjoyable experience, though perhaps a good one for vegetarians to miss.

POD RÓŻĄ

Across the road, on the corner of Św. Tomasza, is the **Pod Różą** hotel ❸, one of the most historic in the city *(see p.113)*. Once the stamping ground of Franz Liszt, among others, besides its fine rooms its oldest section is home to the **Amarone** restaurant, a quiet and very good Italian eatery, see ⑪②.

SZCZEPAŃSKI SQUARE

Walk a further 300m/yds along Św. Tomasza (passing the Church of the Sts John, *see p.35*) on your right, and the **Cherubino** restaurant at no. 15 on your left, see ⑪③, and you arrive at **Plac Szczepański** ❹ (Szczepański Square), named after the baroque Kościół św Szczepana (Church of St Stephen). Built by the Jesuits in the 13th century, the church had been refurbished in a Baroque style by the time it was demolished at the end of the 18th century. The square then became a market place, and is now a car park. Nevertheless, the surrounding buildings include a few interesting sights, not the least of which is the **Morskie Oko** restaurant, unmissable due its huge wooden doors, see ⑪④.

STANISŁAW WYSPIAŃSKI MUSEUM

On the eastern side of the square (the entrance is in fact just around the corner on ul. Szczepańska) is a 17th-century mansion – with 19th-century additions – which provides a distin-guished setting for the **Stanisław Wyspiański Museum** ❺ (Muzeum Stanisława Wyspiańskiego; ul. Szczepańska 11; tel: 012 292 81 83; May–Oct Wed, Sat 10am–7pm, Thur–Fri 10am–4pm, Sun 10am–3pm, Nov–Apr Wed–Thur, Sat–Sun 10am–3pm, Fri 10am–6pm; charge). This was originally the residence of the Szołayski family, who donated the building to the National Museum in 1904. The collection covers the work of Wyspiański (1869–1907), one of Poland's foremost artists, poets and playwrights, and a leading member of the Młoda Polska (Young Poland) Modernist movement.

Collections

The museum includes portraits, landscapes, designs for stage sets and architectural features that appeared in the city's buildings, such as stained glass windows, which can be seen at the Basilica of St Francis of Assisi. There is also a collection of memorabilia, and graphic designs for various editions of his plays.

Above from far left: exhibits in the Museum of Pharmacy; *Portrait of Woman in Armchair* by Wyspiański; Old Theatre on Plac Szczepański *(see p.72).*

Below: *Portrait of Rudolfa Starzewskiego* by Wyspiański.

Bunker Bookshop
The Arts Bunker has an excellent bookshop, stocking reference books on contemporary Polish art and artists, plus prints, postcards and posters.

OLD THEATRE

On the corner of the square, at the junction with ul. Jagiellońska, you'll come across the **Old Theatre** ❻ (Stary Teatr). This, the city's oldest public theatre, was established in 1799 by the renowned actor Mateusz Witkowski. In its mid-19th-century heyday, Helena Modrzejewska starred here in various roles before treading the boards in Warsaw and then the US. The theatre closed in 1893, in the face of competition from the new Słowacki Theatre, and did not reopen until 1945. It was refashioned with wonderful Secessionist details in 1903 by the architects Franciszek Mączyński and Tadeusz Stryjeński, members of the Młoda Polska movement.

If you're ready for a break, there is a neo-Secessionist café in the basement. Needless to say, the lugubrious café, all organic forms and undulating ceiling, attracts the thespian brigade.

You can see another good example of Secessionism in the apartment building at ul. Jagiellońska 2, dating back to 1909. A fine metalwork wreath crowns a stained-glass panel, with decorative balconies overlooking the square. At no. 5 is **Poezja Smaku** restaurant, see ⑪⑤.

TWO ART VENUES

Back on Plac Szczepański, two neighbouring buildings hold exhibitions of modern and contemporary art within very different settings. The aesthetic option is **Palace of Art** ❼ (Pałac Sztuki; no. 4; tel: 012 422 66 16; Mon–Fri 8.15am–6pm, Sat, Sun 10am–6pm; charge), a Secessionist building designed by Franciszek Mączyński, with a highly decorative frieze by Jacek Malczewski that includes busts of Matejko and Wyspiański.

Arts Bunker

The aptly named **Arts Bunker** (Bunkier Sztuki; Plac Szczepański 3a; tel: 012 421 38 40; Tue–Sun 11am–6pm, Thur until 8pm; charge) is virtually the only intrusion of ugly, modern architecture in the

Right: video installation in the Arts Bunker.

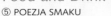

Food and Drink

⑤ **POEZJA SMAKU**
Ul. Jagiellońska 5; tel: 012 292 80 20; daily noon–midnight; €€€
The name of this place means 'Poetry of Taste', and given the richness of many of the dishes on the menu this is not hyperbole. Choose from one of six different dining rooms (and two gardens in summer) and feast on a quality *bigos* (the national dish) and more extravagant treats such as wild boar with red beetroot and dumplings.

city's historic centre. It holds interesting exhibitions of contemporary art.

JÓZEF MEHOFFER HOUSE

Continue west across the Planty and proceed along ul. Krupnicza to reach **Józef Mehoffer House ❽** (Dom Józefa Mehoffera; ul. Krupnicza 26; tel: 012 421 11 43; May–Oct Tue, Wed, Sat 10am–7pm, Thur–Fri 10am–4pm, Sun 10am–3pm, Nov–Apr Wed–Thur, Sat–Sun 10am–3.30pm, Fri 10am–6pm; charge, free on Thur). One of Poland's finest painters, Mehoffer (1869–1946) was a pupil of Matejko and, together with Stanisław Wyspiański, a pioneer of Modernism. In addition to landscapes, portraits and still life, he designed stained-glass windows and polychrome.

Period Interiors

Most of the house is furnished as it was in the artist's day. It's as interesting for its stylish period interiors as for the abundance of Mehoffer's works. The elegant dining room features charcoal portraits and architectural drawings of Krakow such as the Main Market Square in 1903. In the library hangs a 1943 painting of the garden (which can be visited Apr–Oct). The salon has a collection of family portraits, and there are two vast designs for stained-glass windows over the staircase. Secessionist furnishings include linen curtains embroidered with butterflies in Mehoffer's bedroom. By contrast, a Japanese room with scarlet walls and lacquered cabinets is a treasure trove of oriental objets d'art.

Curious Chemists
The city's chemist shops themselves also have some surprising features. There's a wonderful mosaic of a lion at Under the Golden Lion (Pod Złotym Lwem) pharmacy at ul. Długa 4, and an impressive bas-relief at Under the Golden Tiger (Pod Złotym Tygrysem) pharmacy at ul. Szczepańska 1. Under the Golden Elephant (Pod Złotym Słoniem) at pl. Wszystkich Świętych 11 has retained the building's late 19th-century interiors.

Stanisław Wyspiański

Polymath Stanisław Wyspiański (1869–1907; self portrait *below*) was a painter, poet, dramatist, theatre reformer, stage designer and typographer. His colourful and original paintings and stained-glass window designs for the Basilica of St Francis in 1895 signalled a major breakthrough for the Młoda Polska (Young Poland) art movement – an offshoot Art Nouveau, or the Secession, that influenced art for two decades during the Austrian regency in Krakow. Alas, Wyspiański was as troubled as he was talented, and suffered from deep depression, often destroying recently completed work when fits would take hold. He died tragically young, of syphilis in 1907, at the age of 38. His legacy is as rich as his life was short.

GREEN KRAKOW

Escape the busy streets of the Old Town by circumnavigating Krakow's green belt. Follow the route of the old city walls and enjoy landscaped gardens and fine statuary, and explore quirky little side streets.

Fun for Kids
Although the full route may be a little too long for young children, they will love a visit to the Dragon's Cave *(see pp.41 and 78)*, while the many small paths that lead off the main route (especially on the western side of the Planty) are great for impromptu games of hide-and-seek.

DISTANCE 5km (3 miles)
TIME A full day
START/END Obelisk Floriana Straszewskiego
POINTS TO NOTE
Start by the subway leading to the Planty gardens from the main railway station. Though a long walk, there are plenty of benches on which to rest.

The **Planty** is actually a series of individual gardens that form a green horseshoe around the city centre. While short on flowers, they are big on shaded avenues, lawns, water features and monuments. The gardens were created in the 1820s when the Austrian authorities decided to demolish the medieval city walls. Throughout the walk, foundations of the original walls can still be seen, and plaques show where bastions once stood.

NORTHERN PLANTY

Emerging from the railway station subway, you'll see on the left the **Obelisk Floriana Straszewskiego ❶**, a monument that honours the 19th-century senator who was instrumental in planning the layout of the gardens.

Victims of Communist Aggression
From the obelisk, continue along the main footpath in the direction of the Barbican, and you will pass a far smaller monument dedicated to **Victims of Communist Aggression ❷** (Ofiarom Komunistycznej Prowokacji). Unveiled in 1936, this depicts trade union members clashing with the police. It was removed by the Soviets and replaced only in 1989.

Through the trees on the left is the flamboyant late 19th-century **Juliusz Słowacki Theatre** (Teatr im J Słowackiego; *see p.33*), one of the city's leading theatrical venues, modelled unapologetically on the Paris Opera House.

Barbican
Walk another 150m/yds, passing Florian's Gate *(see p.33)* on your left, and you will arrive at the **Barbican ❸** (Barbakan; daily May–Oct 10am–6pm; charge). Benefiting from a 10-year restoration programme in the 1990s, the Barbican is one of Europe's biggest and best-preserved examples of medieval defensive architecture. King Jan Olbracht laid the foundation stone of this circular Gothic building that has walls up to 3.5m (11ft) wide at the base. It was surrounded by a deep moat more than 25m (82ft) wide, and linked to Florian's Gate by *szyja* (the

Below: Commemorated by an obelisk, Florian Straszewski was the man behind the Planty.

neck) – basically a bridge leading over another moat. You can walk around the battlements for fine views across the Planty and the integral courtyard.

Adjoining the final section of the city walls is the rear of the **City Arsenal** (Arsenał Miejski), now part of the Czartoryski Museum.

Above from far left: the Planty is a perfect place to escape from the bustle of the city; Barbican detail; Juliusz Słowacki Theatre.

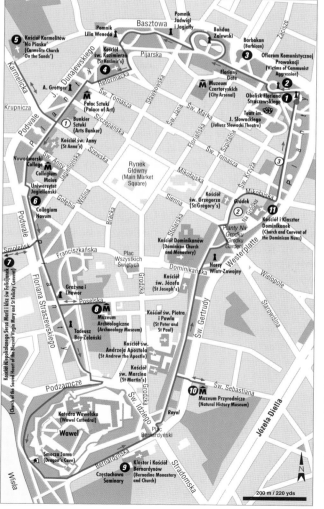

Pomnik Jadwigi i Jagiełły

Basztowa

Pomnik Lilia Weneda

Bohdan Zalewski

Barbakan (Barbican)

5 Kościół Karmelitów 'Na Piasku' (Carmelite Church 'On the Sands')

Kościół św. Kazimierza (St Kasimir's)

Pijarska

3 Ofiarom Komunistycznej Prowokacji (Victims of Communist Aggression)

Karmelicka

4

Reformacka

Floriana Gate

2

A. Grottger

Sw. Tomasza

Muzeum Czartoryskich (City Arsenal)

Obelisk Floriana Straszewskiego

1

Krupnicza

Pałac Sztuki (Palace of Art)

1 Bunkier Sztuki (Arts Bunker)

Podwale

Teatr im. J. Słowackiego (Juliusz Słowacki Theatre)

Kościół św. Anny (St Anna's)

Sw. Anny

Szczepańska

Szewska

Nowodworski College

Collegium Maius Uniwersytet Jagielloński

Rynek Główny (Main Market Square)

Mikołajska

3

6 Collegium Novum

Gołębia

Wiślna

Sienna

Mikołajska

Na Grodzku

Podwale

Bracka

Kościół św. Grzegorza (St Gregory's)

Gródek

2

11 Kościół i Klasztor Dominikanek (Church and Convent of the Dominican Nuns)

Smoleńsk

Franciszkańska

Grodzka

Plac Wszystkich Świętych

Stolarska

Kościół Dominikanów (Dominican Church and Monastery)

Planty Na Grodku (Grodku Garden)

Westerplatte

7

Dominikańska

Narcy Wiatr-Zawojny

Wielopole

Grażyna i Litawor

Poselska

Kościół św. Józefa (St Joseph's)

Starowiślna

Floriana Straszewskiego

8 Muzeum Archeologiczne (Archaeology Museum)

Kościół św. Piotra i Pawła (St Peter and St Paul)

Sw. Gertrudy

Tadeusz Boy-Żeleński

Kościół św. Andrzeja Apostoła (St Andrew the Apostle)

Podzamcze

Kościół św. Marcina (St Martin's)

Sw. Sebastiana

10 Muzeum Przyrodnicze (Natural History Museum)

Józefa Dietla

Katedra Wawelska (Wawel Cathedral)

Sw. Józefa

Grodzka

Royal

Wawel

Plac Bernardyński

Smocza Jama (Dragon's Cave)

Bernardyńska

Stradomska

Wisła

Kościół Niepokalanego Serca Marii i klasz św Felicjanek (Church of the Sacred Heart of the Blessed Virgin Mary and St Felicity Convent)

9 Klasztor i Kościół Bernardynów (Bernadine Monastery and Church)

Częstochowa Seminary

N

200 m / 220 yds

Snack Time
The starting point is a good place in which to pick up a snack, typically from a stall tended by a friendly 'granny'. Recommended street food includes *obwarzanki* (bread rings flavoured with either rock salt or poppy seeds) and *świderki* (literally 'little drills' – sweet, brioche- style bread fingers). For extra sustenance, try a *oscypek* (smoked ewe's-milk cheese that is produced by Highlanders).

Water Features and Monuments

Walking away from the Barbican you'll see one of the largest of the Planty's artificial lakes on your right, where silver birch trees, ponds and a fountain create an atmospheric setting for the 1886 statue of the poet **Bohdan Zalewski**. The lake is home to swans in summer. Crossing ul. Sławkowska, a little further along you will see another 1886 monument, by Oskar Sosnowski, marking the quincentenary of the **Polish-Lithuanian Commonwealth**. It depicts Queen Jadwiga and Duke Władysław Jagiełło. Walk another 200m/yds along the path which runs parallel to ul. Basztowa and you will see Alfred Daun's statue of his muse, **Lilla Weneda**. Daun created a series of statues for Krakow's parks in the early part of the 19th-century; his work can also be seen in Jordan Park (*see p.51*).

WESTERN PLANTY

Just to the southeast is the junction of ul. Pijarska and ul. św Marka. Proceed south along ul. Pijarska and turn right into ul. Reformacka, where on the right-hand side you'll find the **Church of St Kasimir ❹** (Kościół św Kazimierza), a 17th-century Baroque affair with fine Secessionist polychromy.

Cross ul. św Tomasza to ul. Szczepańska and the corner of Szczepański Square. On the left is the flamboyantly elegant Secessionist **Palace of Art** (Pałac Sztuki; *see p.72*); next is the 1960s **Arts Bunker** (Bunkier Sztuki). On the right Wacław Szymanowski's attractive 1901 Secessionist monument to the renowned Krakow painter **Artur Grottger** is set in a semicircular flower bed.

By the junction with ul. Szewska, **Zalipianek Café** (Kawiarnia u Zalipianek) has an attractive open-air terrace with views of the Planty, see ⑪①.

Karmelicka Street and the Carmelite Church

Where the main Planty path crosses ul. Szewska, a worthwhile detour to the walk can be taken along **ul. Karmelicka**, to the right. The street once formed part of the route from Krakow to Łobzów (today merely a suburb of Krakow). It was for a time one of the finest streets in the city, and

Below: snow falls by the Carmelite Church.

Food and Drink 🍴

① **ZALIPIANEK**

ul. Szewska 24; tel: 012 422 29 50; daily 8am–9pm; €€
Historic Cracovian café which serves a fine selection of cakes, bite-sized sandwiches and teas besides some very strong coffee. Perfect for a break while exploring Planty Gardens, the service out on the terrace can be a little slow, but when the view is as good as this, who's rushing?

though its smart 19th-century town houses are today a little faded (and long since divided into smaller flats), they retain a latent elegance.

The Baroque **Carmelite Church and Convent 'On the Sands'** ❺ (Kościół Karmelitów 'Na Piasku') is found at no. 12, some 300m/yds along ul. Karmelicka. The church dates from the 11th century and features the painting of *Our Lady of the Sands*, hence its name. Allegedly an 11th-century Polish duke cured a skin disease by rubbing sand into his wounds at the site, which had been pointed out to him by the Virgin Mary. The church was founded in the 14th century, though the painting – as with much of the rest of the present building – dates from the late 17th century.

Collegium Novum

Picking up the main route again at ul. Szewska, pass St Anna's Church *(see p.53)* and Collegium Nowodworskiego *(see p.54)* on your left, and follow the Planty path as it darts south. In front of Collegium Maius *(see pp.54–5)*, by ul. Gołębia (Pigeon Street), you'll find a small wooded enclave with a statue of Copernicus dating from 1900.

Cross the square and a Matejko portrait of Copernicus *(see p.69)* can be seen in the assembly hall of the adjacent **Collegium Novum** ❻ (ul. Gołębia 24). This neo-Gothic building, which was designed by Feliks Księżarski and built in 1883–7, replaced the Jerusalem College, destroyed in a fire a decade earlier. Its façade features crests of

the Jagiellonian University, and the building is now used as the university's primary administrative centre. Graduation ceremonies take place in its great hall. In 1942 the Nazis arrested 184 academics here whom they had accused of plotting against the occupiers: they all died in Sachsenhausen concentration camp. The college counts King Jan III Sobieski and Pope John Paul II among its alumni.

Church of the Sacred Heart

Continuing in a southerly direction, turn right into ul. Smolensk, where after 100m/yds you will find the 1884 **Church of the Sacred Heart of the Blessed Virgin Mary** ❼ (Kościół Niepokalanego Serca Marii), at no. 6. This is where the late pope prayed when he was Bishop of Krakow. Nuns from the adjoining Convent of St Felicity painted the Stations of the Cross and the mural of Our Lady by the main altar in the 1950s.

TOWARDS WAWEL

Return to the main route, walk along the leafy Planty lane for 250m/yds, crossing ul. Franciszkanska, and look out for a path leading sharply left, which leads to a small square where an 1886 **statue of Grażyna and Litawor** (two characters from 'Grażyna', regarded as one of Adam Mickiewicz's finest poems) is surrounded by trees.

Archaeology Museum

Back on Planty lane, turn left again at ul. Poselska, and head towards the

Above from far left: detail from a 19th-century town house on ul. Karmelicka; Polish-Lithuanian Commonwealth monument; town house gargoyle; Collegium Novum.

Below: the statue of Grażyna and Litawor.

Above from left:
view of Wawel Cathedral and Castle; bas-relief on the façade of the Częstochowa Seminary; Planty fountain.

Bernardine Church
The original Bernardine Church, a 15th-century Romanesque affair, was deliberately destroyed in 1655 on the orders of Polish General Stefan Łodzia Czarniecki to prevent it falling into the hands of the invading Swedes.

Archaeology Museum ❽ at no. 3 (tel: 012 422 71 00; Mon–Wed 9am–2pm, Thur 2–6pm, Fri 10am–2pm, Sun 10am–2pm, July–Aug same hours except Tue 2–6pm; charge except Sun), housed in a former friary of a Carmelite Order. Founded in 1606, this is the oldest Archaeology Museum in Poland, and contains some fine exhibits, including Egyptian mummies and sarcophagi, as well as a thorough history of clothing from 70,000BC to the 14th century.

Upon leaving the museum turn left and head back towards Planty, continuing south with Wawel directly ahead of you. After 50m/yds or so you will you reach a small square containing a monument to the translator and arts critic **Tadeusz Boy-Żelenski** (1874–1941).

The Walls of Wawel

On reaching ul. Podzamcze, turn right and follow the walls of Wawel Royal

Castle all the way round, the tower of Wawel Cathedral *(see p.39)* visible on your left. You will pass Dragon's Cave (Smocza Jama, *see p.41*), after which the path forks. To follow Planty around take the left fork. At the next fork continue straight (rather than turning left) to arrive on ul. Bernardynska. If you find yourself walking steeply up towards Wawel you've gone wrong.

Bernardine Monastery

Walk 300m/yds along ul. Bernardynska, passing the **Częstochowa Seminary ❾** (built in 1928 and featuring a superb bas relief on its façade), and head for the **Bernardine Monastery and Church** (Klasztor i Kościoł Bernardynów; also known as the Reformed Franciscan Church; open only for Mass), next to the seminary at no. 2. The Bernardine Order was established here in the 15th century by the anti-Semitic Giovanni da Capistrano. A wooden church originally stood on the site; the present, Baroque church dates from the 17th century. The church's *Madonna and Child with St Anne* is the only part of the wooden church to remain. Later details include Mehoffer's stained-glass windows depicting the life of St Simon, a 15th-century Bernardine monk.

EASTERN PLANTY

On leaving the church turn right and, after crossing busy ul. Stradomska, turn left before darting right at the first opportunity into the eastern section of the Planty.

Natural History Museum

After 150m/yds, past the Royal Hotel, you should turn right into ul. św Sebastiana for a short detour to the **Natural History Museum 🔟** (Muzeum Przyrodnicze; Mon–Thur 9am–5pm, Fri–Sun 9am–6pm; charge) at no. 9. Housed in a Secessionist, former public bathhouse, the museum was established in 1865 and hosts a decent collection of stuffed birds and insects, though bison – which still run wild in the forests of eastern Poland – are given top billing.

Returning to Planty after visiting the museum you can admire the churches of St Andrew the Apostle *(see p.60)* and Sts Peter and Paul *(see p.59)*; almost as impressive from the rear as from the front as you walk north along the tree-lined lanes towards St Joseph's. Crossing ul. Domikanska, with the Dominican Church *(see p.57)* on your left, you will soon pass a **statue of Narcyz Wiatr-Zawojny**, a Polish colonel shot by the Soviets in 1946. The statue, made by Bronislaw Chromy, was erected in 1992.

Church of the Domincan Nuns

Crossing ul. Sienna and entering what is known as the **Grodku Garden** (Planty Na Gródku), turn left and follow ul. św Krzyża as it meanders around, with St Gregory's Church on your left. As ul. św Krzyża gives way to ul. Mikołajska you will see the entrance of the **Church and Convent of the Dominican Nuns 1️⃣1️⃣** (Kościół NMP Śnieżnej i Klasztor Dominikanek; open only for Mass) at no. 21. Founded by Duchess Anna Lubomirska in the 1630s, it possesses elegant Baroque interiors, with an ornamental vaulted ceiling and a neo-Baroque main altar. The 17th-century painting of *Matka Boska Śnieżna* (Our Lady of the Snow, to whom the church is dedicated), was a gift from Pope Urban VIII, and (of course) is said to have miraculous powers of healing. When the Swedes besieged Krakow in the 17th century, Our Lady of the Snow appeared above the convent, shielding it from attack with her cape. The astonished Swedes abandoned their siege, and the convent survived.

Just east across ul. Na Gródku is the Gródek Hotel, whose restaurant **Cul de Sac**, see 🍴②, is great for dinner. To the north on ul. św Marka is the **Zakopianka** café and restaurant, with alfresco tables overlooking the Planty, see 🍴③.

From the convent return to ul. Mikołajska and head north along the Planty path to return to the Florian Straszewski Obelisk.

Galeria Krakowska

Shoppers might want to end the walk with a retail trip to the Galeria Krakowska, the city's largest shopping mall, which can be reached via the subway leading to the railway station. Find the shopping centre – which is difficult to miss – between the station and the city's main post office, on ul. Lubicz.

Food and Drink 🍴

② CUL DE SAC

Ul. Na Gródku 4 (Gródek Hotel); tel: 012 431 20 41; daily noon–11pm; €€€€
A highlight of any visit to Krakow is a visit to this exquisite restaurant, which besides offering opulent surroundings goes to great lengths to introduce diners to new flavours and new twists on classic Polish cooking. Try dishes featuring roast pheasant or guinea fowl, and worry about the cost at a later date.

③ ZAKOPIANKA

Ul. św Marka 34; tel: 012 421 40 45; daily 8am–11pm; €€€
Not the cheapest café in the city by any means, but a thoroughly enjoyable place to spend time while circumnavigating Planty. It can get quite lively in the early evening as a drinks venue for commuters who pop in before heading off to the station. Great views from the terrace.

PODGÓRZE: THE JEWISH GHETTO

Visit Krakow's former Jewish ghetto, which for two years during World War II was a place of horrific suffering and brutality. Much forgotten for decades, its historical importance is only now being fully recognised.

Pharmicist Hero

Tadeusz Pankiewicz was the only gentile resident of the ghetto. He operated his pharmacy *(see p.81)* throughout World War II, helping the Jews any way he could. He gave sedatives to Jewish children to keep them quiet during Gestapo raids, and let the ghetto's undergound movement use the pharmacy as a meeting and hiding place.

DISTANCE 3.5km (2¼ miles)
TIME A half day
START Plac Bohaterów Getta
END Oskar Schindler Factory
POINTS TO NOTE

Trams 9, 13 and 23 run from Poczta Główny on the edge of the Old Town through Kazimierz and over the Wisla into Podgórze. To follow the route taken by the Jews when the Nazis created the ghetto in 1941, walk over the Most Powstancow Sląskich.

On 21 March 1941 the Nazis established a Jewish ghetto in Podgórze, a district of Krakow into which they herded the 20,000 Jews from Kazimierz *(see p.43)* who had not yet been deported to the concentration camps. Forced to leave at less than a day's notice, the Jews were allowed one cartload of possessions per family, and were crowded into the area between Plac Bohaterów Getta and Rynek Podgórski. From Podgórze Jews were sent to Auschwitz or Płaszów. Only about 2,000 of Kazimierz's pre-war Jewish population survived.

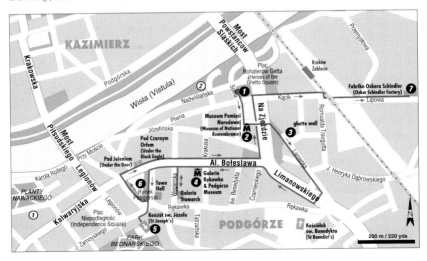

HEROES OF THE GHETTO SQUARE

If you cross Powstancow Sląskich Bridge on foot you will arrive at **Plac Bohaterów Getta** ❶ (Heroes of the Ghetto Square). The square was the centre of the Jewish ghetto and features a poignant memorial to those killed, in the form of 70 randomly scattered chairs in bronze. The memorial was designed by Piotr Lewicki and Kazimierz Latak, and is officially called *Nowy Plac Zgody* (New Concordia Square), invoking the name by which the square was known when it served as the heart of the ghetto, Concordia. The chairs themselves are a reference to a passage in a novel by Tadeusz Pankiewicz, proprietor of the Pharmacy Under the Eagles *(see margin left)*, describing the furniture lying around the ghetto after its liquidation in 1943.

Museum of National Remembrance

Straight ahead of you is Pankiewicz's former pharmacy, in the far southwest corner of the square. Now home to the **Museum of National Remembrance** ❷ (Muzeum Pamieci Narodowej; Plac Bohaterów Getta 18; tel: 021 656 56 25; Tue–Thur 9.30am–4pm, Fri 10am–5pm, Sat 9.30am–4pm, closed Sun–Mon; charge), it was kept throughout the war by Pankiewicz – the ghetto's only non-Jewish inhabitant, who refused to leave his home. The museum is small, but features some extraordinary photos and a couple of shocking films of day-to-day ghetto life.

Ghetto Wall

Turn right as you exit the pharmacy, cross Na Zjeżdzie and head through the small park to ul. Lwowska 25, where you will see one of just two parts of the original **ghetto wall** ❸ which once enclosed the entire area (there was only one entrance and exit, on Plac Bohaterów Getta). The wall is marked with a small plaque commemorating the ghetto's victims. It reads: *'Here they lived, suffered and perished at the hands of Hitler's executioners. From here they began their final journey to the death camps.'*

Concentration Camp

Set up in 1942 as a slave labour camp, Płazsów concentration camp was the fiefdom of Amon Goeth, the brutal camp commandant portrayed by Ralph Fiennes in *Schindler's List*. Though not an extermination camp per se, death from disease and execution were daily occurrences, and more than 10,000 people are thought to have died here. Now overgrown, you can wander around the few remains of Płazsów by taking tram nos 9, 13 or 32 three stops south from Plac Bohaterów Getta. Climb up the hill on foot and take a right into ul. Jerozolimska. There is a large memorial to the dead in a clearing *(pictured below)*, while Goeth's crumbling former home can be seen at ul. Heltman 22.

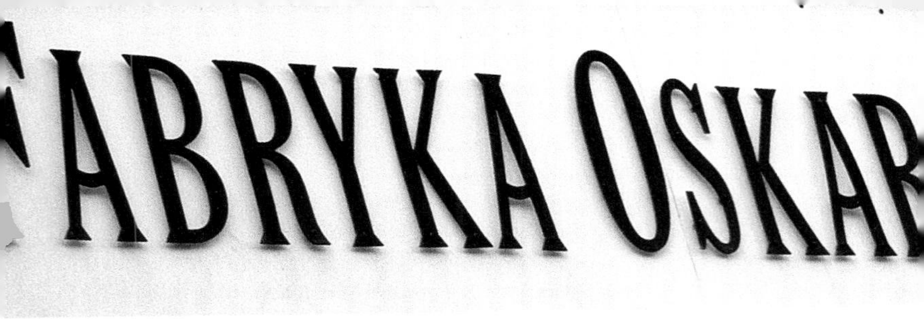

![FABRYKA OSKAR](heading image showing sign text "FABRYKA OSKAR")

Below: St Joseph's.

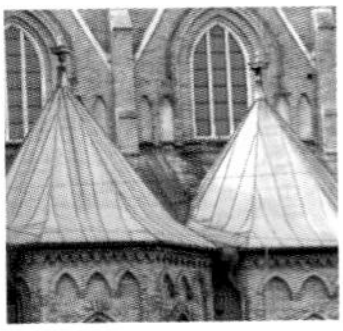

THE MAIN STREET

Head south along ul. Lwowska until you reach al. Bolesława Limanowskiego, Podgórze's main street. Just south of here, at the top of a hill, is **St Benedict's Church** (Kościół św Benedykta; closed to visitors), which dates from the 11th century, and a fort.

Turn right and follow al. Limanowskiego as it curves around for about 300m/yds. On the corner with ul. Krakusa at no. 13, you will see the **Galeria Rękawka** ❹ (tel: 021 656 36 65; Mon–Sat 10am–6pm), an outstanding contemporary art gallery which also houses the small **Podgórze Museum** (same hours as gallery), a collection of photos and a short film about the area, before, during and after World War II. From here you can take a left into ul. Węgierska, where on the left at no. 5 is another excellent art gallery, the **Galeria Stamarch** (Mon–Fri 10am–5pm, Sat 10am–2pm), housed inside a converted former synagogue.

Continue along al. Limanowskiego. You will see the towering neo-Gothic

St Joseph's Church ❺ (Kościół św Józefa; daily 7am–6pm, closed during Mass) to the left, at the far end of **Rynek Podgórski** ❻, Podgórze's former market square. Built in 1905–9 to designs by Jan Sas-Zubrzyckiego, the church dominates the square and is topped with a green spire that would not look out of place in Disneyland. It is less impressive inside. On the eastern side of the square is the 19th-century former Podgórze **town hall**, next to which once stood another factory which made use of Jewish slave labour.

On the square's northern side are two former inns, built in the mid-18th century: **Under the Deer** (Pod Jeleniem) is at no. 12, **Under the Black Eagle** (Pod Czarnym Orłem) is at no. 13.

For good food, however, you will need to walk a little further west, along Kalwarijska, past **Plac Niepodległości** (Independence Square) to **Ogniem I Mieczem** on Planty Nawackiego, see ⑪①. For drinks, head back towards the river, and **After Work** is at the Qubus Hotel on ul. Nadwiślańska, see ⑪②.

SCHINDLER FACTORY

Retrace your steps to Plac Bohaterów Getta, cross the square and head west on ul. Kącik. Continue under the railway bridge along ul. Lipowa, where at no. 4 is the **Oskar Schindler Factory** ❼ (Fabrika Oskara Schindler; Mon–Sat 10am–4pm; charge), the very building in which Oskar Schindler at first exploited and then protected more than 1,000 Jews. Pass through the original Schindler Gates, and head inside to find

SCHINDLERA · EMALIA

a recreation of Schindler's office and a 10-minute film recalling Schindler's life. For years there have been plans to convert the factory into a much larger Schindler Museum and Memorial, but due to an ongoing dispute over the ownership of the building and the land, these plans are currently suspended.

Oskar Schindler

Oskar Schindler (1908–74) was born to a wealthy family in the Sudetenland (in the present-day Czech Republic), and was childhood friends with the Jewish family next door. He moved to Krakow at the outbreak of the war (allegedly to avoid conscription – settlers moving east were exempt), and purchased a struggling enamel factory from a local Pole, which he staffed with cheap Jewish labour. Producing bomb casings for the Nazi war effort, Schindler grew rich, yet he frittered away much of his money on women and black-market goods, which he used to buy the loyalty of local SS officers. After witnessing the liquidation of the Podgórze ghetto in 1943, Schindler vowed to do what he could for 'his' Jews, and managed to have his factory declared a sub-camp of the nearby Płaszów concentration camp. As the Red Army closed in on Krakow, however, his factory was forced to close and his Jews scheduled for deportation to an extermination camp. Schindler managed to persuade the authorities to let him take 1,200 workers to a new factory at Brunnlitz, close to his home town. It was at this point he was forced to draw up his now famous list of workers who would join him. Brunnlitz was liberated by the Red Army on 9 May 1945, though Schindler had fled the night before: a Nazi party member since 1930, he would almost certainly have been shot. He fled first to Spain before living as a farmer in Argentina until 1958, when he returned to Germany. At the time of his death in 1974, in Frankfurt, he was bankrupt and living off the charity of those he had saved.

Roman Polanski

One survivor of the ghetto was film director Roman Polanski, who, as an 11-year old boy, escaped through a hole in the ghetto wall during its liquidation. He survived the rest of the war by hiding in the forests that surround Krakow, living off the good will of Polish families. In 2002 he won an Oscar for Best Director for *The Pianist*, set in the Warsaw ghetto.

Left: Schindler in his factory – a still from *Schindler's List*, with Liam Neeson and Ben Kingsley.

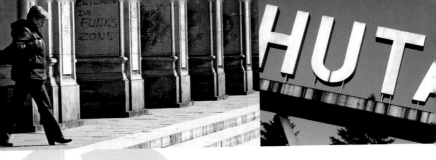

NOWA HUTA

Take a tram to this unique 1950s experiment in social engineering: a town and steelworks built 10km (6 miles) east of the city centre to redress what the Soviet Union saw as Krakow's 'class imbalance'.

Tiring Tours

Though both Nowa Huta's and Krakow's tourist offices *(see pp.85 and 108)* suggest routes for seeing the town, neither is to be recommended as they involve a great deal of walking between sights. Walking to and from the steelworks, for example, will take the best part of an hour.

DISTANCE 3km (2 miles)
TIME A half day
START Plac Centralny
END Arka Pana Church
POINTS TO NOTE

To get to Nowa Huta you should take tram no. 4 from the Poczta Główny stop on the eastern edge of the Old Town in Krakow, or tram no. 15 from outside the city's main railway station. The journey takes no more than 35 minutes. A taxi takes considerably less and costs around 20zł each way.

Nowa Huta is one of only two towns in the world designed and built to an entirely Socialist Realist concept (the other is Magnitogorsk, in Russia in the former USSR). Conceived by Poland's Communist authorities in collusion with the Soviet Union at the end of the 1940s, Nowa Huta (which means New Steelworks) was constructed to create at once both a modern steelworks to support the industrialisation of southern Poland, and a proletarian base in Krakow: until then Krakow was seen (somewhat mistakenly) as a city without a working class. Built mainly from 1949 to 1953, the architecture of Nowa Huta is a mix of neo-Renaissance, neoclassical and Utilitarian. Ignored by visitors to Krakow until recently, the town has attracted something of a cult following in recent years both for Communist nostalgics and for students of architecture. For the casual visitor it provides a telling insight into how the 'utopia' many Communists aspired to create might have looked.

CENTRAL SQUARE

If coming from Krakow by tram, get off at **Plac Centralny ❶**, the centre of Nowa Huta. As you will see immediately, all streets fan out from here, and

the scene – of five almost identical, wide, tree-lined avenues and smart blocks – is immediately impressive. Designed by a collective (what else?) of Polish architects, the square was the first part of Nowa Huta to be completed, in 1952. Looking around you will note that the southern side of the square lacks any buildings: this was not deliberate. A giant cultural centre was planned for the site but was never built.

Before heading further into Nowa Huta, cross over to the southern side and walk east for 100m/yds along al. Jana Pawła II to take a look at the blocks of the **Na Skarpie ❷** district. Built in the 1970s, they are considered by most residents to be an eyesore.

THE MAIN STREET

Walking back to Plac Centralny, head directly north along **al. Róż**, Nowa Huta's primary thoroughfare. After 50m/yds it widens to form a large square, often used today for concerts by bands both local and foreign making use of the town's increasing popularity. The neoclassical apartment blocks which line the square are the finest in the town and were reserved for the highest echelons of steelwork management. Most have arched, Renaissance-style walkways. Today the apartments are sought after by property speculators. The taller building on your left, on the corner of al. Przyjazni, and sporting a rather sublime loggia, is Nowa Huta's **former town hall ❸**.

Cross al. Przyjazni and dart right into one of the many gorgeous little **parks**

that dot the town. Nowa Huta was designed so that a third of its area would be green space, and does suggest that the architects wanted to make life for residents as pleasant as possible. Walk to the other side of the park, where there are benches if you need a rest, and head into the **Tourist Information Centre** on os. Słoneczne. Inside is the **Nowa Huta Museum ❹** (Muzeum Narodwe Oddział Nowa Huta; os. Słoneczne 16; Mon–Sat 9am–4pm, Wed 10am–5pm; charge except Wed), a small space which features changing exhibitions on the town's history and culture.

LUDOWY THEATRE

Head north a further 100m/yds along al. Róż to the junction with al. Żeromskiego. Turn left and head northwest, taking the right-hand fork after 50m/yds. On your left, set back from the street, is the **Ludowy Theatre ❺** (Teatr Ludowy; os. Teatralne 34), a low-rise yet still gargantuan building that is one of many in Nowa Huta sadly showing signs of neglect. Completed in 1955, the theatre has long since been associated with avant-garde productions. Inside the theatre is the **Café Lura**, one of Nowa Huta's few food and drink options, see ⓧⓘ *(p.86)*.

ARMED FORCES MUSEUM

Cross the street and the tank that faces you marks the entrance to the **Museum of the Armed Forces ❻** (Muzeum Czynu Zbrojnego; os. Górali 23; Tue–Fri 10am–3pm), a rather touching

Churches of Mogiła
Southeast of Nowa Huta is the tiny, ancient settlement of Mogiła, home to a pair of remarkable churches on either side of ul. Klasztorna. The first, the St Wenceslas Church *(pictured above)* in the Cistercian Abbey, dates from 1266 and features intricate folk art motifs on its walls and ceilings. Across the street, the 15th-century St Bartholomew's is the only wooden church in Krakow.

Above from left: stained glass in Arka Pana Church; Nowa Huta's steelworks; street named after Pope John Paul II.

Still Making Steel
At its peak in the 1970s the Nowa Huta steelworks were producing more than 7 million tonnes of steel annually. Today the steelworks are the second-largest in Europe.

Below: the exterior of Arka Pana Church.

museum devoted to those from the Nowa Huta area who have fought and died for Poland. It is worth dragging a Pole along if you can to explain what the exhibits are all about, though those depicting life in Poland under the Nazis are sadly all too self-explanatory.

ARKA PANA CHURCH

Exit the museum and turn right, walking a further 300m/yds to Plac Włosika, where you will find the startling **Arka Pana Church** ❼ (Kościół Arka Pana; ul. Obrońców Krzyża 1; tel: 012 644 06 24; daily 6am–6pm, closed during Mass), the first church to be built in Nowa Huta, between 1967 and 1977. Designing a socialist utopia meant that the original architects of Nowa Huta

had no room for any churches in their plans, and for decades the authorities refused repeated calls from locals to build one. Finally, Nowa Huta's faithful took things into their own hands and began construction of the church. Designed by Cracovian Wojciech Pietrzyk to resemble Noah's Ark, the Arka Pana was built brick by brick, work often stopping for months on end due to a lack of materials. It was finally completed in 1977; Karol Wojtyła's election as pope (Wojtyła had blessed the site as Bishop of Krakow when construction began) prevented its demolition by angry authorities.

Set over two levels, the church has bizarre decorations: a huge figure of Chirst flying to Heaven, a tabernacle containing a fragment of rutile brought

---

Food and Drink

① CAFÉ LURA
Os. Teatralne 34 (inside Teatr Ludowy); tel: 012 680 21 26; times vary; €€
Coffee and a super collection of cakes, though only open when there's something on at the theatre – usually every day, from early afternoon to late at night, but you may want to call ahead first.

② SANTORINI
Ul. Bulwarowa 35b; tel: 012 644 91 11; daily 10am–11pm; €€
This little place is about the closest Nowa Huta currently comes to having a real restaurant. In the town's hotel, it offers surprisingly good if simple food, even though the old Polish fault of offering far more dishes on the menu than they actually have is well adhered to here. It really is your only decent option.

back from the Moon by the crew of Apollo 11, and a statue dedicated to *Our Lady the Armoured* made from 10kg (22lbs) of shrapnel removed from Polish soldiers wounded at Monte Cassino.

THE STEELWORKS

From the church turn left and walk back 50m/yds to the junction with Bieńczycka, from where tram no. 1 will take you back to the centre of Krakow. However, for many people a visit to Nowa Huta is not complete without a trip to the town's *raison d'être*: the steelworks. To get there, head back to Plac Centralny, and take tram no. 4 to the Kombinat stop, directly in front of the steelworks' entrance. You can't miss it: enormous letters framed by monumental twin buildings (the administration centre) tell you that this is **Huta im. Sendzimira** (Szenzimir Steelworks). Nowadays owned by the Arcelor-Mittal group, during Communism the steelworks carried the name of Lenin, and its workers were famously militant *(see box)*.

You can't actually see that much, as the steelworks are currently off limits to the public, though a visitors' centre is planned to open in 2010.

If you are set on eating something in Nowa Huta, your only real option is the **Santorini** restaurant at the hotel of the same name, see ⑪②. When returning from the steelworks, get off the tram one stop before Plac Centralny (the Struga stop), and take bus no. 123 to os. Zielone.

Aviation Museum

Just west of Nowa Huta is the Polish Aviation Museum (Muzeum Lotnictwa Polskiego; al. Jana Pawła II 39; <www. muzeumlotnictwa.pl>; Mon–Fri 9am–5pm, Sat–Sun 10am–4pm; charge). Alongside the rusty Soviet-era MIG fighters are some real highlights, including one of the world's few remaining Spitfires in perfect condition. To get there take tram nos 4, 5 or 15 to the AWF stop. If you're coming from the city centre then walk back the way you came a short distance – the museum is set back from the road through a small wooded park. If in doubt, ask a local to point the way.

A City of Rebels

Nowa Huta was designed to be a city of the proletariat, with its inhabitants (at its peak there were 200,000; today's population is slightly less) all loyal supporters of the Communist party. Like much about Nowa Huta, however, not everything went according to plan. The workers of the steel plant have often been a major thorn in the side of Poland's authorities, both before and after the fall of Communism, most notably in 1981.

As Nowa Huta expanded in the 1970s and huge tobacco and cement factories also opened nearby, new housing had to be built quickly. As a result, building standards dropped and the size of apartments shrank. Allied to the general drop in living standards throughout Poland in the late 1970s, it was no surprise that Nowa Huta's workers came out on strike in support of the Solidarity movement in 1981. The authorities had to use force (though stopped short of using live ammunition) to quell the riots.

Ironically, the fall of Communism and the onset of capitalism may see the death of Nowa Huta. The steelworks face a precarious future, and their closure would be a terrible blow to the town.

ZAKOPANE

This is a pretty holiday resort in Poland's Carpathians; it's home to the ethnic Górals, and for more than a century has been a traditional retreat for intellectuals and a popular winter sports venue.

DISTANCE 100km (62 miles) one way from Krakow; town centre tour: 3.5km (2 miles)

TIME A full day

START Grand Hotel Stamary

END Gubałówka

POINTS TO NOTE

Most of Zakopane's sights can just about be visited on a day trip from Krakow, although if you want to hike or ski then you should stay at least one night. Zakopane can be reached from Krakow by train or bus. The bus is recommended, as the train is painfully slow. There are a number of private bus companies of varying comfort operating the route; they depart from Krakow's main bus station and deposit passengers at the Grand Hotel Stamary. The journey by bus takes just over two hours in good weather.

Below: wooden buildings with carvings are typical of the region.

Food and Drink 🍴

① GRAND CAFÉ STAMARY

Ul. Kościuszki 19 (Grand Hotel Stamary); tel: 018 202 45 10; daily 9am–11pm; www.stamary.pl; €€€
After a long bus ride from Krakow, you may wish to refuel with some coffee and cake in this café, conveniently located in the castle-like Grand Hotel Stamary beside the bus station.

The enchanting little town of **Zakopane**, one of Poland's most popular tourist resorts, is known for its beautiful mountain scenery in summer and prime skiing in winter. Set at the foot of the Tatra Mountains, Zakopane was, from around the 16th century, a Góral sheep-farming village. The Górals are a small ethnic group of highlanders from the Podhale and Pieniny regions, to which they are thought to have migrated from the north of Poland in the 13th century. They speak their own dialect and maintain traditional customs, including folk music and dancing. Zakopane's restaurants and concert halls often feature performances by Góral choirs and dance troupes. Vernacular architecture is characterised by wooden buildings adorned with carvings and painted rustic motifs – the churches are particularly beautiful.

A Symbol of Resistance

Poland 'discovered' Zakopane in the 1870s when a Warsaw doctor, Tytus Chałubiński, visited what was then a village. The first hotel was built in 1885 to accommodate a specific clientele: artists and intellectuals inspired by the Górals' indomitable sense of independence. The Górals were seen as a symbol of resistance to occupations by Prussia,

Russia and Austria. Zakopane became a bohemian centre at the start of the 20th century, with a cultural guest list starring the likes of Nobel Prize-winning novelist Henryk Sienkiewicz and concert pianist Ignacy Paderewski. Some of Poland's leading artists established permanent homes here, and elements of Góral culture began to appear in the work of composers such as Karol Szymanowski and writers like Jan Kasprowicz. The painter, architect and critic Stanisław Witkiewicz was a key figure in propagating the 'Zakopane style'.

A WALK AROUND THE TOWN CENTRE

Having arrived at the bus station in front of the **Grand Hotel Stamary** ❶, you might want to relax for a while in the hotel's **Grand Café**, see

🍴①. From here, turn right and head along ul. Kościuszki as it passes through the town centre's largest park, the **Równień Krupówka** ❷.

Torture and Tatra Museums

Cross al. 3 Maja and continue to ul. Krupówki, the town's busy main thoroughfare. Turn left, and some 200m/yds along you'll come to the small but gory **Torture Museum** ❸ (ul. Krupówki 30; tel: 018 201 50 66; daily 10am–9pm; charge), featuring a whole host of medieval instruments of torture.

Far more pleasant is the **Tatra Museum** ❹ (Muzeum Tatrzańskie; tel: 018 201 52 05; Tue–Sat 9am–5pm, Sun 9am–3pm; charge), back along ul. Krupówki at no. 10. It has a fine collection of folk art, and more besides: two reconstructions of ancient mountaintop dwellings delight kids of all ages.

Above from far left:
wooden houses; Zakopane sits at the foot of the Tatras; cowbells for sale.

Tourist Information
Next door to the Grand Hotel Stamary, at ul. Kosciuski 17, is Zakopane's excellent tourist information centre. It sells good hiking maps as well as a decent guide to the resort's complicated ski-run network and lift-ticket system.

Billy Goats Gruff

A museum devoted to *Koziołek Matołek*, a much loved billy goat and hero of Polish children's stories, can be visited at ul. Tetmajera 15 (tel: 018 201 22 63; Wed–Sun 10.30am–1.30pm). The museum is housed in the former home of *Koziołek Matołek*'s creator, Kornel Makuszyński (1884–1953).

Two Parish Churches

On the other side of the road is the 1877–96 neo-Romanesque **Krupówki Parish Church 5** (Krupówki Kościół Parafialny). Witkiewicz designed its **Chapels of John the Baptist and Our Lady Mary of the Rosary** (Kaplica Jana Chrzciciela and Matki Bożej Różańcowej), as well as the stained-glass windows and polychromy, in the Zakopane style.

Turn right into ul. Krupówki and then left into ul. Kościeliska, a street which will give you an idea of the town's architectural idiosyncrasies. On your right is the town's oldest church, the mid-19th-century **Old Parish Church 6** (Stary Kościół Farny). In the church's cemetery you'll find the tombstones of several famous figures, including Witkiewicz and Chałubiński, as well as that of Helena Marusarzowna, a Polish ski champion shot by the Nazis in 1944 for being a member of the Polish resistance.

Villa Koliba

About 100m/yds further along is the **Villa Koliba 7** (Willa Koliba; ul. Kościeliska 18; tel: 018 201 36 02; Wed–Sat 9am–5pm, Sun 9am–3pm; charge),

built in 1893 by Witkiewicz and based on a highlander's cottage. The villa is one of the few original 19th-century Zakopane hunting lodges to have survived, and is decorated in the typically sumptuous style of the period.

Karol Szymanowski Museum

From here, cross the road and walk along ul. Stolarczyka to ul. Kasprusie. To your right, on the other side of the road, will be the Villa Atma's **Karol Szymanowski Museum 8** (ul. Kasprusie 19; tel: 018 201 34 93; Tue–Sun 10am–3.30pm; charge except Thur). The villa was home in the 1920s to Szymanowski (1882–1937) – the most important Polish composer of the first half of the 20th century.

UP TO GUBAŁÓWKA

Walking back to the town centre along ul. Kaprusie, cross the small park, pass through the town's large **market**, and head up on to Na Gubałówka. At no. 2 is a wonderful shop and **gallery** selling paintings of Zakopane and its mountains (do not expect bargains) as well as genuine local painted glass (Zakopane has a long history of glass-painting).

Funicular and Food

A short distance up the hill is a **funicular** (daily, Dec–Apr 8am–4pm, May–Oct 10am–5.30pm; closed Nov for maintenance; charge), which whisks skiers, bobsledders and hikers up to **Gubałówka 9**, once a tiny mountain village, now a mini resort-within-a-

Below: local faces.

resort. In winter there are some short and easy ski runs here, while in summer there are pony rides for children and long hikes across the Tatras.

The **Gubałówka** restaurant at the top of the funicular is a scenic spot to eat, see ⑪②, or a place to rest tired legs if you have walked up the mountain (the route is steep; it can be done by the very fit in around an hour. It is not recommended for young children or the elderly, or for anyone in bad weather).

Alternatively, head back into town to ul. Krupówki for hearty Górale cooking at **Karczma Sabala**, see ⑪③.

NATIONAL PARK MUSEUM

At the far south of the resort, opposite a neglected stadium, is the **Tatra National Park Museum** (TPN, Muzeum Tatrzańskiego Parku Narodowego; ul. Chałubińskiego 42a, tel: 018 206 32 03; Mon–Sat 8am–3pm) which has some good exhibits (in Polish only) on the environmental threat to the Tatra region, and efforts to save the mountains from further development and deforestation. Next door in a tiny wooden hut is a **tourist information centre**.

Food and Drink 🍴

② GUBAŁÓWKA

Ul. Gubałówka 2; tel: 018 206 36 30; daily 10am–7pm; €€€

At the top of the Gubałówka, this mountain retreat offers cheap and cheerful Polish dishes in a rather bizarre wood and glass box-like building. Still, the views out over the mountains are terrific, the waitresses are dressed like Heidi and nobody has ever been known to complain, except that there are no free tables. A popular wedding venue for locals, it can be closed for private occasions on high summer weekends.

③ KARCZMA SABALA

Ul. Krupówki 11; tel: 018 201 50 92; daily 11am–11pm; €€

Places like this are what Poland's mountains are all about. A super wooden villa (there are hotel rooms on the upper floors), good food, a great atmosphere and decent prices. The food is local: *Górale* specialities such as *patelnia bacowska*, a rich lamb stew, are a feature of the menu. The staff are friendly and speak perfect English.

Hiking and Skiing

Zakopane is known for summers that can last until October, and for its green spaces; some 12 percent of the land within the town limits is forest, and a vast meadow fills the heart of the town. The region is popular with hikers – numerous well-marked trails lead to the gorgeous Alpine scenery of the Tatra Mountains. All routes are well marked, using familiar international hiking symbols, but you should not set off without a good map, available at tourist information centres in the town, as well as in good Krakow bookshops.

While hiking is unquestionably popular, of all Zakopane's 3 million annual visitors, most come to ski (at busy times it can appear that they have all arrived at once). There is usually good snow from December to mid-April, but though there is some good skiing to be had the overall experience can be a little disappointing. The ski runs are split into four separate areas (none of which interlink), and there is no Zakopane ski area lift pass. The best skiing is on Kasprowy Wierch to the south of the resort, accessed by an antiquated cable car. Queues for the cable car are long; so long, in fact, that you can reserve your place the day before at the ticket office. Local environmentalists have blocked plans for a new, high-speed gondola to the summit. See also www.zakopane.pl.

AUSCHWITZ

The infamous Nazi death camp is now a Unesco World Heritage Site and museum. From 1940–45 between 1.1 and 1.5 million people were murdered here, almost a quarter of all those killed in the Holocaust.

Taxi from Birkenau
If you complete your tour of Birkenau long before one of the buses is due to leave, take a taxi – numerous taxis are lined up at the entrance. A trip back to Auschwitz should cost about €5.

Below: details from the main camp.

DISTANCE 60km (37 miles) west of Krakow

TIME A full day

POINTS TO NOTE

Oświęcim is served by regular buses from Krakow's bus station (every 20 minutes from 7am to around 8.45pm). The journey takes around 90 minutes, meaning that Auschwitz can be visited on a long day trip. The bus stops in the car park opposite the camp memorial reception area. Buses returning to Krakow also depart from here (the last bus leaves at 6.58pm).

You can buy overpriced snacks and drinks from stalls round the main entrance to Auschwitz, but none serve anything resembling a meal (visiting the site leaves most people feeling physically sick). Come prepared with bottles of water, as in high summer walking around the vast, open camp at Birkenau can get very hot.

The town of **Oświęcim** (Auschwitz) will always be synonymous with the Holocaust. It is now an industrial centre south of Katowice, Poland's key industrial conurbation. The site of a castle in the 12th century, it became the capital of an independent dukedom in 1317 and part of Poland in 1457. In the years of Poland's partition (1772–1918) the town was part of Austria.

Creation of Auschwitz-Birkenau

Shortly after they invaded Poland in 1939, the Nazis built the Auschwitz-Birkenau concentration camp. The largest such complex in the country, it comprised two camps covering an area of 172ha (425 acres). Auschwitz was a slave-labour camp largely reserved for political prisoners, members of the resistance and other 'opponents' of the Nazi regime – mainly Poles and Germans; Auschwitz II-Birkenau, opened in 1943, was solely used as an extermination camp.

The Killings

Transported in cattle trucks from all over Europe, between 1.1 and 1.5 million prisoners from 28 nations lost their lives here. Though the vast majority of victims were Jews, there were numerous Polish, Russian and gypsy inmates, too. Many died as a

result of slave labour, hunger, illness and torture. The genocide peaked in 1942, when the gas chambers were killing up to 20,000 people per day.

Liberated by the Red Army

Before retreating in 1944, the Nazis began destroying the evidence of their horrific crimes. They detonated the crematoria and some camp buildings, but did not have enough time to destroy the gas chambers. The camp was liberated by Russia's Red Army in 1945.

AUSCHWITZ I

Auschwitz-Birkenau (Apr, Oct 8am–5pm, May, Sept 8am–6pm, June–Aug 8am–7pm, Mar, Nov 8am–4pm, Dec–Feb 8am–3pm; tel: 033 844 80 03; children under 12 should not watch the introductory film, though they are admitted; entrance to the camps is free, there is a charge for the introductory film and for guided tours) was established as a national museum in 1947, and in 1979 it was listed by Unesco as a World Heritage Site.

A visit to Auschwitz begins with a visit to the **reception and information centre**. Here you can enquire about **guided tours**, as well as watch the chilling **introductory film** (in English at 10am, 11am and 3pm). You should purchase a copy of the official guide book, which comes complete with the suggested route around both camps. Auschwitz and Auschwitz II (Birkenau) are 3km (2 miles) apart: a free shuttle bus connects the two, departing every hour on the hour throughout the day.

Arbeit Macht Frei

From the reception, make your way past the former SS Guard House and through the notorious **camp entrance gate**, complete with the infamous camp motto, *Arbeit Macht Frei* (Work Makes You Free). Passing the former kitchens on your right, where the camp orchestra would play as prisoners were marched to work, in front of you is **Block 4**, which contains the first main exhibition, outlining the story of the camp, as well as the creation of Zyklon B, the gas used to kill so many prisoners. In a room at the rear are the remains of more than 7 tonnes of human hair, shorn from prisoners as they entered the camp and originally intended for German clothing factories but abandoned along with the camp in January 1945.

Next door is **Block 5**, which displays belongings stripped from prisoners as they arrived. Most poignant are the children's shoes and toys, while the piles of glasses and artificial limbs are equally harrowing. Daily life in Auschwitz is covered in **Blocks 6 and 7**, and includes exhibitions of camp prisoner art.

The Wall of Death

At the far end of the camp (between Blocks 10 and 11 – the last blocks on your left) is the **Wall of Death**, where daily prisoners were shot for breaking the smallest of camp regulations. **Block 10** (closed to visitors) was itself an awful place: medical experiments were carried out here on mainly female prisoners. Many died as a result of the experiments, while others were left with permanent disabilities.

Above from far left: glasses that once belonged to inmates; the infamous motto that greeted prisoners upon arrived.

Camp Motto
Arbeit Macht Frei (Work Makes You Free) was not, as many people believe, a sick joke intended to fool Jews entering Auschwitz into believing that if they worked hard enough they would be freed. Instead it draws on the Nietzschean idea that only through hard labour can man genuinely feel free.

Block 11 was the camp's prison, a dreaded place in which many of the cells were so small that prisoners could neither sit down or stand up, and which were also pitch black. Few survived in here for more than a few days. Though many of the cells were destroyed, you can visit that of Father Kolbe, a Polish priest who died here of starvation after sacrificing his life so that a Jewish inmate could live. It was in the cellars of Block 11 that the Nazis carried out their first experiments with Zyklon B, in 1941.

National Memorials

From Block 11 visitors turn right and head back towards the main entrance, passing various blocks given over to

National Memorials. These are designed and maintained by memorial groups from many of the countries whose citizens died here, and change frequently. The Dutch exhibition is usually the most moving, while most recently a permanent memorial to the Roma (gypsies) who died here has also been created. You should ask at the reception centre which exhibitions are currently open and on display as you arrive at the camp.

THE GAS CHAMBER

After walking through **Roll Call Square**, where – until the camp's population became unmanageable – Roll Call would be held three times a day,

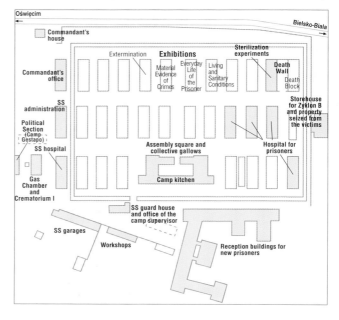

Above: the Gates of Hell.

continue to the end of the row of blocks to the entrance to a reconstruction of Auschwitz's original **gas chamber and crematoria**. The gas chamber functioned from 1941–3, and was used to put to death those prisoners who were no longer fit for work. After the creation of the extermination camp at **Auschwitz II-Birkenau** in 1943, the gas chamber at Auschwitz was dismantled and the building used as an air-raid shelter by the SS.

The **gallows** which stands in front of the gas chamber was that used to execute camp commandant Rudolf Hoess in 1947. From here, follow the path 200m/yds back to the reception centre, from where you can catch the bus to Auschwitz II-Birkenau.

AUSCHWITZ II-BIRKENAU

If you take the bus to Birkenau you will be deposited at the **Gates of Hell**, one of the few parts of the camp left intact. Featured in a number of films – including *Schindler's List* – which have been set in the camp, they are now almost as infamous as the *Arbeit Macht Frei* gates in Auschwitz I, and when viewed from afar they are a chilling sight. Follow the original railway tracks through gates to the site of the unloading ramp, where the trains carrying Jews from all over Europe would arrive, and where selection would take place: those fit for work would be sent for processing, while those declared unfit would immediately be sent to the camp's gas chambers.

In terms of camp remains, there is very little to see at Birkenau, and there is no suggested route. It is a place of reflection and remembrance. Most visitors, however, choose to walk the length of the unloading ramp to the remains of the gas chamber and crematoria, where there is a simple memorial to the victims of the camp. To the left of the ramp are two reconstructed womens' barracks, which show the appalling conditions inmates had to endure. As many as 600 people shared one barrack house.

From the gas chamber, walk 300m/yds northwest to the so-called sauna (another reconstruction) where those chosen for work were disinfected before being assigned to barracks which were rife with disease.

From here, walk past the Ash Pond – one of many pits on the outskirts of the camp where the ashes of prisoners were dumped – and trace the outline of the camp back to the Gates of Hell: its scale is terrifying. Even more so is the knowledge that it was to be extended. The vast area behind the Ash Pond was known as Mexico, intended for expansion but never completed.

WIELICZKA SALT MINE

Explore a centuries-old subterranean world as you adventure through one of the Continent's oldest working salt mines, with museums, galleries, chapels, burial grounds and even an underground restaurant.

DISTANCE (Mine tour) 3.5km (2 miles)

TIME A half day

POINTS TO NOTE

Wieliczka is 15km (9.3 miles) from Krakow. The town can be reached by minibuses, which depart from in front of Krakow's main train station (Dworcek Główny) every 10 minutes throughout the day. Alternatively, there are frequent trains, though the journey time is longer due to frequent stops. It's a good idea to wear sensible footwear.

Below: St Kinga's Chapel *(see p.98).*

The town of Wieliczka, which received its charter in 1289, developed around the highly lucrative salt-mining trade. The salt was initially obtained from various springs that bubbled up in the area, a process so successful that, in the 14th and 15th centuries, this was one of the Continent's most important mining towns. A feature on Unesco's World Cultural Heritage List since 1978, **Wieliczka Salt Mines** (Kopalnia Soli Wieliczka; ul. Daniłowiczlo 10; tel: 012 278 73 02; www.kopalnia.pl; daily Apr–Oct 7.30am–7.30pm, Nov–Mar 8am–5pm; by guided tour only – available in different languages – individual tourists must wait for a tour group to be assembled; charge) is Poland's and possibly the world's oldest working salt mine. Tickets, books and souvenirs can also be purchased in Krakow at ul. Wiślna 12a (tel: 012 426 20 50).

Visiting the Mine

Every year, Wieliczka receives over a million visitors. It has a 3.5km (2-mile) tourist trail that descends to level three – some 135m (443ft) underground – making for a moderately strenuous two-hour tour, the descent into the mine being by stairway (although lift access can be arranged). If you have a fear of confined spaces, this is probably not an expedition for you. It's possible to leave the tour at only a few locations, and even if you do get out early, you may need to wait your turn for the cramped cage lift to get you back up to ground level.

THE FIRST LEVEL

After being sorted into language groups in the reception area (which can involve a wait of up to an hour), you descend the 378 steps of the **Daniłowicz Shaft**, sunk in 1635, to level one. The shaft itself continues to level six, at a depth of 243 metres (800ft). At the bottom, you will be cramped into a tiny space for five minutes while the guide presents some basic information about the mine. From here you are led to the **Copernicus Chamber**, a huge room dedicated to the astronomer Copernicus, who visited the mine in the 15th century while a student at the Jagellonian University. A memorial to Copernicus takes pride of place, sculpted and brought here in 1973. Next you pass through the Baroque **St Anthony's Chapel**, which hosted its first service in 1698: it is the oldest of the mine's chapels. Almost all of the chapel's decorations and sculptures are made of salt.

There are more salt sculptures in the **Janowice Chamber** next door, while the **Burnt Chamber** is a chilling reminder of the dangers of salt mining: an explosion here in the 19th century killed a number of miners. Today a rather frightening (though totally safe) light-and-sound show demonstrates how susceptible the mine was to fire before they discovered how to extract methane gas safely. The tight **Sielec Chamber** is the next you will visit, where you can see a number of tools used by salt miners over the centuries.

Moving to the other side of the mine, the enormous and impressive **Casimir the Great Chamber** displays an original horse-powered harness used to haul salt from lower levels, yet is merely a taster of what comes next: the **Pieskowa Skała Chamber**, one of the largest in the mine, which links level one with level two, 35m (115ft) below. Be warned: the stairs are very steep in places.

THE SECOND LEVEL

In the **Kunegunda Traverse** the original wooden drains which carried out excess water have been preserved, alongside waxworks of miners hauling salt through the tunnels. You will then pass through the **Kunegunda Gallery** and see a bizarre collection of salt dwarves, carved by abstract Polish artist Stefan Kozik, which are lit up in bright colours as Polish children's music is played over loudspeakers.

The **Holy Cross Chapel** features a Baroque wooden crucifix dating from

Labyrinthine Mine
Dating back to the 12th – or, according to some sources, the 10th – century, the mine area consists of a number of attractions. It comprises nine separate levels that reach a depth of 327m (1,073ft). The salt lodes are 1km wide and 6km (3½ miles) long, and the total, labyrinthine length of all the mine's galleries, chambers and tunnels extends to more than 300km (186 miles).

Above from left: altar in St Kinga's Chapel; souvenir lights from the mine; St John's Chapel.

the 17th century, after which you will visit **St Kinga's Chapel**, probably the most impressive of the mine's places of worship. It features a number of bas-reliefs, all carved in salt by talented miners and depicting scenes from the New Testament, as well as a pulpit (also in salt) in the approximate shape of Wawel Hill.

From the chapel you are led downhill towards the **Erazm Barącz Chamber**, home to one of the mine's salt lakes. The water here is 9m (30ft) deep. As you walk around the precarious wooden gallery you will wonder how on earth it was built. Continuing downhill, through the **Michałowice** and **Drozdowice Chambers**, you arrive at the deep **Wiemar Chamber**, carved in the 16th century and named for the Prince of Weimar who visited in the 17th century. There are some impressive salt sculptures in the various

recesses and a deep brine lake at the bottom; note that the staircase which hugs the walls as you descend to level three is as steep as they come.

THE THIRD LEVEL

A monument commemorating Józef Piłsudski (a legendary Polish World War I general and politician who in 1926-35 was the virtual dictator of Poland), carved in rock salt by the miner sculptor Stanisław Anioł in 1997, dominates the upper part of the **Piłsudski Chamber**. One of the first parts of the mine to be opened up as a tourist trail (by the Austrians in the 1830s), it leads past the Poniatowski Traverse to the 36m (118ft) high **Staszic Chamber**, dedicated to Stanisław Staszic, a 19th-century geologist of whom there is a bust (in salt of course) in a recess at the top of the chamber, from where a glass lift brings you down to the bottom of the chamber.

The **Poniatowski Traverse** features a waxwork recreation of the mine's safety warden telling miners to abandon a part of the mine. The mine's wardens had a crucial job in monitoring gas levels and assessing fire risk. The last part of the guided tour, you are next taken into the **Witold Budryk Chamber**, today a restaurant, see 🍴①. At this point you are 125m (410ft) below the surface.

Leaving the restaurant, you will pass through the **Warsaw Chamber** which, with its neat rows of hanging chandeliers, looks much like a ballroom. In fact it is. It also hosts

Food and Drink 🍴
① WIELICZKA PODZIEMNA RESTAURACJA
Wieliczka Salt Mine, Level Three; tel: 012 278 73 24; open until 90 minutes after the last tour ends; €€€
The restaurant at the mine could be one of Europe's great tourist traps, but thankfully the mine's management have kept it simple and relatively cheap. The salty, briny atmosphere of the mine stimulates the appetite, so prepare to tuck into huge portions of Polish food, such as borsch, roast lamb stew and breaded pork in creamy mushroom sauce. Groups can pre-order food so it is ready and waiting at the end of their tour.

Geological Tour
Geologists can take part in a special 6km (4-mile) extended tour of the mine, which includes a number of chambers where the geological make-up of the Wielicka deposits can be studied. You must be over 18 to take the tour and must sign a declaration that you are in perfect health.

conferences, parties (the New Year's Eve party here is legendary) and sometimes even concerts. In the next chamber there is a souvenir shop and a post office, after which you need to descend further, along the wide staircase of the **Prinzinger Drift**, to the very bottom of the third level. The charming wooden altar of the otherwise unimpressive **St John's Chapel** is on your left, the last part of the mine open to the public. From here you will see signs pointing ahead towards the main shaft, and the lift back to the surface.

Underground Sanatorium

Since the mid-19th century, when salt baths were first recognised for their potential as healing agents, Wieliczka has also enjoyed the benefits of a **sanatorium**. Today its underground chambers are still used as a location for the treatment of respiratory illnesses, particularly asthma, and allergies. The sanatorium offers a short (and free) tour of its facilities to the general public, though note that to stay here you need a recommendation from a Polish doctor.

SALTMASTER'S CASTLE

While you are in Wieliczka, it is also well worth visiting the neighbouring **Saltmaster's Castle** (Museum Żup Krakowskich w Zamku Żupnym; May–Sept Mon–Sun 10am–5pm, Oct–Apr Mon, Wed–Sat 9am–2.30pm; charge). As you leave the mine, the castle grounds are directly opposite. Originally

a 13th-century fortress that was turned into a Renaissance castle in the 16th century, this is the country's sole example of medieval architecture relating to salt mining and trading. To see an exhibition focusing on the ancient and early medieval history of Wieliczka, you have to go underground once more – it's in the original 13th- to 15th-century cellars. The 16th-century Gothic hall, with a vaulted ceiling supported by a single pilaster, is hung with portraits of the castle's former salt lords. A collection of salt cellars reflects various styles from the 18th to the 20th centuries. The display also features Polish and other European porcelain, and showcases the work of the genre's biggest names, such as Meissen.

Other buildings within the castle complex include a 14th-century Gothic bastion and defensive walls, a warehouse, guardhouse and kitchen.

Wieliczka's Churches
In addition to the salt mine and castle, this historic town has a traditional market square and two churches of note. St Clement's Church (Kościół św Klemensa) dates from the 14th century and is especially worth visiting for its Baroque chapel. At the 16th-century St Sebastian's Church (Kościół św Sebastiana) you'll find Włodzimierz Tetmajer's wonderful early 20th-century polychromy of sacral and Gothic motif.

Left: salt carving.

DIRECTORY

A user-friendly alphabetical listing of practical information, plus hand-picked hotels and restaurants, clearly organised by area, to suit all budgets and tastes.

A

ADDRESSES

In Poland, the name of the street always comes first, followed by the house or building number. Streets are usually numbered odd on one side, even on the other, though in many parts of Old Krakow, rather more arbitrary systems are used.

B

BUSINESS HOURS

Banks open early, usually at 8am, and stay open until around 6pm. All banks are closed at weekends. During the week, shops open at 9am or 10am and stay open until about 6pm, with shorter hours on Saturdays; most are closed on Sundays. Exceptions include shops inside big shopping malls, and markets; the latter are open by 5am and generally stay open until the middle of the afternoon. Museums and galleries generally open at 10am, and close any time from 2pm to 6pm. Most museums are closed on Mondays.

C

CLIMATE

Winters are crisp and snowy, with December and January typically cold, damp and foggy. Don't let this put you off: when covered with snow, Krakow looks magnificent, and the surrounding attractions, such as Zakopane, Poland's premier ski resort, are in full swing. Summers are usually hot and sunny from May to September, though September and October can be very wet. During the winter a warm coat, hat and gloves are required; even during the summer a light raincoat and waterproof shoes are a sensible precaution.

CRIME AND SAFETY

Although Krakow is generally safe, all cities pose a potential threat, so take sensible precautions. Don't leave coats hanging around with valuables in the pockets, or leave your mobile phone on a table. Take care when travelling on busy trams and in any crowded space, especially outdoor concerts. As in any city of this size, exercise caution when walking around late at night. Stick to well-lit streets, and if in doubt, use a taxi. Areas to be avoided late at night include the main railway station, the Planty gardens and ul. Westerplatte.

CUSTOMS REGULATIONS

Since Poland joined the EU in 2004, duty-free allowances no longer apply to travellers arriving from or leaving for other EU countries. However, some EU countries have imposed their own limits on what can be imported from Poland: the UK, for example, limits cigarette imports to 800.

Dogs and cats may be brought into the country, providing they are accompanied by an official vaccination certificate from a vet, which is less than 12 months old and valid at least three

Above from far
left: façades on ul.
Kanonicza; view
from the Town
Hall Tower.

weeks prior to arrival. (This document should be translated into Polish.)

Antiques and works of art produced in Poland that are not registered and not older than 55 years can be freely exported. If permission is necessary, it can be applied for at the Wojewódzki Urząd Ochrony Zabytków, ul. Podchorążych 1 (tel: 012 426 10 10). Keep in mind that this can take a few months and may involve extra cost in the form of taxes. Good antique dealers should take care of the paperwork for you.

Ogólnopolski Związek Inwalidów (The Polish Association of Invalids), Al. Daszynskiego 22; tel: 012 422 80 63.

Polski Związek Gluchych (The Polish Association for the Deaf), ul. św. Jana 18; tel: 012 422 39 94.

Polskie Towarzystwo Walki z Kalectwem (Polish Association Campaigning on Behalf of the Disabled), ul. Dunajewskiego 5; tel: 012 422 28 11.

Polski Związek Niewidomych (The Polish Association for the Blind), ul. Babińiskiego 29; tel: 012 262 53 14.

D

DISABLED TRAVELLERS

All new buildings and building renovation work in Poland must meet rigid EU standards concerning the provision of facilities for the disabled. Places in Krakow such as the airport, many hotels and quite a few restaurants are now up to Western standards. However, the cobbled streets of the Old Town and most of the best sights within it remain hard work for wheelchair users and travellers with other disabilities. The same also applies for Wawel, Kazimierz and every other destination in this guidebook. Wheelchair users can get around the city fairly easily on most forms of public transport, though older trams are still difficult to access. All new 'bendy' buses are designed for wheelchairs, as are tram nos 8, 34, 36 and 38.

For detailed information about facilities and services for the disabled and disadvantaged, contact one of the following organisations:

E

ELECTRICITY

Electricity in Poland is 220v AC, 50 Hz. Sockets are the standard round, two-pin European variety. Those from the UK, US and outside Continental Europe need to bring an adaptor.

EMBASSIES/CONSULATES

Consulates (in Krakow)

UK: ul. św. Anny 9; tel: 012 311 00 00; www.britishembassy.pl.

US: ul. Stolarska 9; tel: 012 424 51 00; http://poland.usembassy.gov.

Embassies (in Warsaw)

Australia: ul. Nowogrodzka 11; tel: 022 521 34 44; www.australia.pl.

Canada: ul. Matejki 1/5; tel: 022 584 31 00; www.canada.pl.

New Zealand: al. Ujazdowskie 51; tel: 022 521 05 00.

Republic of Ireland: ul. Mysia 5; tel: 022 849 66 33; www.irlandia.pl.

House Names
Before modern
numbering systems
became wide-
spread, houses
were known by a
peculiar charac-
teristic of their
design or their
location. Hence the
plethora of hotels,
restaurants and bars
still prefixed Pod
and U. Pod in Polish
means 'Under' (as
in Pod Różą –
Under the Cover of
Heaven) and U
means 'At' (as in U
Babci Maliny – At
Granny Malina's).

South Africa: ul. Koszykowa 54; tel: 022 625 62 28; www. southafrica.pl.

EMERGENCY NUMBERS

In an emergency, call 999 for an ambulance, 997 for police or 998 for the fire brigade. Alternatively, call directory enquiries 118 913 and ask for the nearest hospital casualty department. From a mobile phone call 112 for general emergencies.

GAY TRAVELLERS

Catholic Poland is a largely conservative country when it comes to social mores, with a far from enlightened attitude to members of its gay community. That said, Krakow's city authorities have in recent years been more open to the gay community than those in Warsaw, where gays suffer from semi-official harassment. The age of consent for gays, as well as heterosexuals, is 15. A handy gay guide to the city can be found by following the Krakow links at www.inyourpocket.com.

HEALTH

EU nationals: UK and EU citizens with a valid European Health Insurance Card (EHIC; available from post offices or online at www.ehic.org.uk in the UK) can receive free treatment, although private medical insurance is recommended. State health care in Poland is underfunded and poor. Should you need to use their services, bear in mind that salaries for state medical staff are low, and that 'gifts' are common, often being necessary to ensure that patients are seen to.

North Americans: You will need to take out medical insurance before travelling. While emergency treatment is technically free, all peripheries (such as ambulances, hospital stays and medicines) have to be paid for.

An English-speaking medical emergency and ambulance telephone service (tel: 012 424 42 00) is available 24 hours a day. Centrum Medicover (tel: 9677) operates a network of medical centres in Poland's major cities, including Krakow. Medicover has English-speaking staff, a broad range of specialists and an ambulance service. Its programme includes home visits, and it will treat non-members. Medical services are also provided by Falck (tel: 9675) and Scanmed (tel: 012 629 88 00).

Dentists: Dentists who speak foreign languages can be booked at the private clinic Dental America, pl. Szczepański 3 (tel: 012 421 89 48), and Dentamed, ul. Na Zjezdzie 13 (tel: 012 259 80 00).

Pharmacies: There are numerous pharmacies *(Apteka)* throughout the city, offering a 24-hour service, including ul. Kapelanka 56, and ul. Galla 26. For information on all-night pharmacies, call 012 661 22 40.

Water: It is better to drink bottled than tap water; locals do. In addition to bigger-name brands, mineral waters from Polish spas are readily available.

I

INTERNET

Among several internet cafés in the centre is Garinet at ul. Floriańska 18 (tel: 012 423 22 33), which is open from 9am–midnight and offers plenty of high-speed machines at 4zł per hour. International courier companies include UPS, ul. Kosiarzy 6, tel: 012 614 55 55.

L

LANGUAGE

Polish, along with Czech, Slovakian and Serbian, is one of the western Slavic languages, and is written using Latin letters with the occasional diacritic thrown in to confuse non-speakers. The Poles excel in running consonants together in such a way as to terrify all but the hardiest of polyglots. The good news is that the majority of people working in the tourist industry in Kraków speak good English and/or German. Attempting a few basic words is always a nice thing to do and is appreciated by the locals. A list of simple words and phrases can be found on the pull-out map that accompanies this guide. As a general rule, the accent falls on the penultimate syllable.

M

MAPS

Free maps can be picked up in tourist information centres, hotels, bars, restaurants and cafés. A good map of Krakow is Compass's 1:20,000 scale edition, which covers the city in detail, lists public transport routes and has the only decent map of Nowa Huta in print.

MEDIA

Newspapers: Polish broadsheets include *Dziennik Polski* (Polish Daily) and *Gazeta Wyborcza* (The Electorate's Newspaper). Of the various English-language listings magazines available, the best is *Krakow In Your Pocket* (5zł), widely available from newsagent kiosks, hotels and Empik outlets. A number of Polish publications carry English-language sections, such as *Karnet Krakow Cultural Events* (3zł), and *Miesiąc w Krakowie* (4zł), which has 'This Month in Krakow' printed on the reverse side. The English can be sub-standard or even unintelligible, however. Empik (Rynek Główny 5) has a fine selection of European and American newspapers and magazines.

Television: Most hotels have satellite TV offering English-language stations such as CNN and BBC World.

Radio: Local radio stations include Radio Krakow on 101.6 FM, and Jazz Radio 101 FM. Radio Polonia is available at www.polskieradio.pl/polonia.

MONEY

Currency: Poland's currency comprises złoty (paper notes and coins) and groszy (coins): 100 groszy equals 1 złoty. Groszy coins come in denominations of 1, 2, 5, 10, 20 and 50. Smaller denominations of złoty (1, 2 and 5 złoty) are coins; higher denominations (10, 20, 50, 100 and 200 złoty) are in the form of paper notes.

Bureaux de change: The best place to change money is in a bank, and there are many in the city centre, all offering similar exchange rates. While exchange kiosks and counters (marked *Kantor*) throughout the city offer better rates, they also apply large commission charges. Beware signs declaring 'No Commission': these usually apply only when Polish currency is being sold.

Cash machines: Scattered throughout the city, cash machines remain the cheapest way to get your hands on local currency. You'll find one at the Unicredit-Pekao Bank (Rynek Główny 31), at numerous other sites in the square (nos 21, 25, 47) and at ul. Floriańska 6.

Credit cards: Internationally established credit cards, including American Express, Visa and MasterCard, are accepted by numerous hotels, restaurants and shops. Don't expect smaller establishments to accept credit cards, particularly not for minimal sums.

Cash advances on credit cards can be arranged at a number of banks, including Unicredit-Pekao, Rynek Główny 31. Be sure to bring your passport. There's an American Express and exchange counter at the Orbis travel agent, Rynek Główny 41. You can also cash travellers cheques here and receive Western Union transfers.

POST

Post offices: There are two main post offices in the city centre. One is located by the main railway and bus stations, at ul. Lubicz 4. This is open 24 hours a day all week. The post office at ul. Westerplatte 20 (tel: 012 422 03 22) is open daily 7.30am–8.30pm, Sat 8am–2pm, Sun 9am–2pm. The public telephone boxes are accessible 24 hours per day, all week. There's also a small post office inside Wawel's main ticket office (open daily 9am–4pm), which is never busy and has English-speaking staff.

Stamps for postcards and letters abroad cost 2.40zł, or 1.30zł if you're sending them within Poland. Postboxes are scattered around the city and are red with a yellow post horn set against a blue background.

PUBLIC HOLIDAYS

1 January – New Year's Day
March/April (variable) – Easter
    Monday
1 May – Labour Day
3 May – Constitution Day
June (variable) – Corpus Christi
15 August – Feast of the Assumption

1 November – All Saints' Day
11 November – Independence Day
25 December – Christmas Day
26 December – St Stephen's Day

RELIGION

The vast majority of Poles are Roman Catholic. A Roman Catholic Mass is said in English at 10.30am on Sundays at Kościół św Idziego (on ul. Grodzka).

Though less common, Krakow also has churches and houses of worship for other denominations and faiths. These include Kościół św Marcina (Church of St Martin, Lutheran Congregation) on ul. Grodzka 58, Baptystów (Baptist church) on ul. Wyspiańskiego 4, the Methodist Church on ul. Długa 3 and for Jews, there's Kazimierz's Remuh Synagogue on ul. Szeroka 40.

T

TELEPHONES

Phone numbers: To call Krakow from outside the country, dial your international access code followed by 48 for Poland and the subscriber number minus the initial 0. The 012 at the start of a Krakow number is both part of the number and the code for the city. If you're calling Krakow from anywhere in Poland on a landline you simply dial the 10-digit number. The same applies for calling a landline from a Polish mobile with the exception of Plus GSM, which requires the dropping of

the first 0. To get a line out of Poland, dial 00 plus whatever you need after that for the country in question (Australia 61, UK 44, US and Canada 1). If using a US phone credit card, use the following numbers: AT&T – 0 0800 111 11 11, MCI – 0 0800 111 21 22, Sprint – 0 0800 111 31 15.

National operator, tel: 912, international operator, tel: 901.

Mobile phones: Avoid roaming costs by putting a local prepaid SIM card in your mobile phone. Several companies now offer extremely cheap start-up packages for less than 10zł, with top-up cards costing 5zł and upwards. Both can be bought from shops and kiosks around the city as well as the airport, bus and railway stations and the Empik bookshop listed under Media.

Public telephones: The combined internet and mobile phone revolution has all but seen the death of public telephones in Poland. If you can actually find one, a Krakow public telephone is either yellow or silver and works using prepaid cards in various denominations bought from post offices and newsagent kiosks.

TIME ZONES

Polish time is one hour ahead of GMT.

TIPPING

It is customary to tip restaurant staff, taxi drivers and hotel staff, such as porters, around 10–15 percent. Note that when paying in a restaurant, if you

Above from far left: all dressed up for Easter Monday; tipping in restaurants is customary; postal service sign.

say 'thank you' when handing over the money the waiter will assume that he may keep the change. To make sure you get your change back say *'prosze'* as you hand over the money.

TOILETS

Not only is there a shortage of public toilets in Krakow but, whether it's a public convenience, or in a café or restaurant, the user usually has to pay for the privilege. Vigilant attendants demand that you cough up the cash as per posted prices – usually anything up to 2zł.

TOUR OPERATORS

Polonium Travel (300 London Road, Sheffield; tel: 0114 250 89 89) specialises in holidays to Poland, from ski packages to cosmetic surgery trips.

Regent Holidays (Froomsgate House, Rupert Street, Bristol; tel: 0845 277 33 17) is a long-time specialist in Eastern Europe and offers package and tailor-made city breaks to Krakow.

TOURIST INFORMATION

Offical Krakow City Tourist Office
ul. Szpitalna 25; tel: 012 432 01 10; www.karnet.krakow.pl; open 9am–5pm.

Małopolska Region Tourist Information Office
Rynek Główny 1–3 (within the Cloth Hall); tel: 012 421 77 06; www.mcit.pl; open May–Oct Mon–Fri 8am–8pm, Sat–Sun 10am–4pm, Nov–Apr Mon–Fri 9am–6pm, Sat–Sun 10am–2pm.

For additional information on cultural events you should visit the Centrum Informacji Kulturalnej (Cultural Information Centre) at ul. św. Jana 2; tel: 012 421 77 87; open Mon–Sat 10am–6pm.

You can get information on Jewish-related events from the Jewish Cultural Information Office located at Kazimierz, Centrum Kultury Żydowskiej, ul. Meiselsa 17; tel: 012 430 64 49; fax: 012-430 6497; www.judaica.pl; open Mon–Fri 10am–6pm, Sat–Sun 10am–2pm. Tourist information on Kazimierz is also available at ul. Józefa 7; tel: 012 422 04 71; open Mon–Fri 9am–5pm.

UK: Polish National Tourist Office, Westgate House, West Gate, London W5 1YY; tel: 0870 067 50 10; fax: 0870-067 50 11; www.visitpoland.org.

US: Polish National Tourist Office, 5 Marine View Plaza, Hoboken, New Jersey, NJ 07030; tel: 201 420 99 10; fax: 201 584 91 53; www.polandtour.org.

TRANSPORT

Arrival

By Air: Krakow's John Paul II International Airport is the second-busiest airport in Poland. It is served by direct flights to and from many European cities throughout the year. Flight time from London is just over two hours. Seasonal direct flights operate from distant cities such as Chicago and New York. Additionally, many European and international routes travel to Warsaw's Okęcie Airport, from which there are regular domestic flights to Balice.

By Rail: There are frequent express services to Krakow from various European cities, including Berlin, Budapest, Frankfurt, Prague and Vienna. There is also a regular train service from London to Warsaw, with express trains throughout the day from Warsaw to Krakow (the fastest journey time is around 2 hours and 45 minutes, but you need to make a prior reservation for such express services). For details of trains from Krakow, tel: 94 36 or 004 822 511 00 03 if calling from outside Poland.

Train station information desks may not be staffed by English-speakers, but the colour-coded timetables are fairly easy to follow. The yellow timetable is for departures *(odjazdy)*, the white one for arrivals *(przyjazdy)*. Express trains usually feature the prefix 'ex', and direct trains are indicated as *pospieszny*. Trains marked *osobowy* are slow, sometimes very slow. The main railway station is within easy walking distance of the historic centre, though the traffic system obliges taxis leaving the terminus to take a slightly more circuitous route to the centre. Train tickets can also be purchased from travel agents.

By Road: Coach travel is very cheap in Poland. In Krakow, coaches leave from the bus station at pl. Kolejowy by the main station. Various routes are offered by PKS, the state-owned coach company (for information on coach services from Krakow; tel: 030 030 01 50 or 012 393 52 62). More modern, privately-owned operators include Eurolines Polska (tel: 032 351 20 20). The journey from Krakow to Warsaw can be long because coaches often stop at a number of cities en route.

Airport

Krakow's John Paul II International (Balice) Airport (ul. Kapitana Medweckiego 1; tel: 012 639 30 00; www.lotnisko-balice.pl), 18km (11 miles) east of the city, is small, modern and user-friendly. After passing through passport control and customs, you'll find a small combined arrivals and departures hall on the ground floor, where ATMs and a currency-exchange kiosk (open Mon–Sat 7.45am–8.30pm, Sun 7.45am–7pm) are located, plus a few kiosks where you can buy a Polish SIM card to put in your mobile phone *(see p.107)*.

Getting to the city: The best options are by taxi or train. Ignore the taxi touts and head outside where you'll find plenty of official PT taxis (tel: 91 91) waiting. Make sure the metre is running and expect to pay between 30zł and 50zł. Alternatively, outside the main airport doors is a free bus that takes you to a railway platform where a train runs direct to the city's central train station. Journey time is 14 minutes, and tickets cost either 4zł or 8zł, depending on where you buy your ticket. The service runs regularly every day from around 4am until 11pm. An information desk inside the main terminal building will help you with any other enquiries.

Transport within Krakow

Public transport in Krakow is both cheap and reliable. The fabulous tram

Above from far left: train station clock; tourist information sign; tucking into some candyfloss; taxis are useful for journeys beyond the mainly pedestrianised town centre.

system provides the perfect way of getting around, from 5am to 11pm. Tram tickets cost 2.50zł per ride on one tram over any distance. Better value are 24-hour, 48-hour and 72-hour tickets, costing 10.40zł, 18.80zł and 25zł respectively. Buy them from most kiosks, or anywhere you see a 'Sprzeda Biletów MPK' sign. Tickets must be validated in one of the yellow machines when boarding. Watch a local do it first. People travelling on a single 2.50zł ticket who are in possession of items bigger than 20 by 40 by 60cm (8 by 16 by 24in) need to buy a ticket for that as well (though note few people actually do).

Be careful when getting off trams in the city centre, where they share the roads with cars: you're essentially stepping down into traffic, and drivers do not always give tram passengers priority.

For bus and tram information, tel: 9150.

Train: The main railway station, just a short walk from the historic centre, is Krakow Główny, pl. Jezioranksiego 3, tel: 012 393 15 80. You can catch a train from here to the Auschwitz-Birkenau concentration camp and to Krakow Płaszów, in the Płaszów district, where there are train connections to the Wieliczka salt mine.

Taxi: Although the town centre is essentially pedestrianised, taxis do have access. There are cab ranks around Main Market Square, not that it's very practical or even necessary to use taxis

to get around the centre. Radio taxis, which can be booked by phone, are generally cheaper than taxis from ranks, though the latter are not very expensive. For longer journeys, negotiate the fare with the driver before departure. The following are reliable cab companies:

Euro Taxi, tel: 012 96 64

Express Taxi, tel: 012 96 25

Mega Taxi, tel: 012 96 25

Radio Taxi, tel: 012 91 91

Expect to pay around 5zł per kilometre.

Car rental: Krakow's compact size makes hiring a car more trouble than it's worth. However, for visiting other destinations, a car can be a good idea.

Arrangements and conditions for car hire are similar to those in other countries. The minimum age requirement is 21, and you must have been in possession of a valid licence for at least one year. US and Canadian licences are accepted, as are international driving licences. Ask if collision damage waiver insurance is included in the price.

The following companies all have websites in English, and Europcar and Hertz have offices at the airport:

Avis: ul. Lubicz 23; tel: 012 629 61 08; www.avis.pl.

Cracowrent: ul. Kamieńskiego 41; tel: 012 265 26 50; www.cracowrent.pl.

Europcar: ul. Szlak 2; tel: 012 633 77 73; www.europcar.com.pl.

Hertz: al. Focha 1 (inside the Cracovia Hotel); tel: 012 429 62 62; www. hertz.co.pl.

Joka: ul. Starowiślna 13; tel: 060 154 53 68; www.joka.com.pl.

National: ul. Głowackiego 22 (inside the Demel hotel); tel: 012 636 86 30; www.nationalcar.com.pl.

Rentacar: ul. Piłsudskiego 19; tel: 012 618 43 30; www.e-rentacar.pl.

Sixt: ul. Kapitana Medweckiego 1 (airport); tel: 012 639 32 16; www.sixt.pl.

Driving: It's a sobering fact that Polish traffic fatality figures are among the worst in Europe, a testament to the appalling condition of the roads and the often unsafe driving practices of the locals. Poles drive on the right-hand side of the road.

For those who insist on driving in Krakow, be warned that roadworks are everywhere. If you find yourself following a tram on a stretch of road that doesn't have a separate, fenced-off area for them, proceed with caution. You are expected to stop when trams do, regardless of what lane you're in, as people will be getting on and off, and will be doing so via the road you are driving down.

You can drive in Poland on an EU or US licence. Dipped headlights must be switched on at all times year-round; seat belts are compulsory front and back and the maximum blood-alcohol limit is 0.02 percent.

Speed limits are 130km/h (80mph) on motorways, 110km/h (69mph) on dual carriageways, 100km/h (60mph) on single carriageways, 90km/h (55mph) outside of urban areas, and 50km/h (30mph) in built-up areas. You may be fined on the spot for speeding.

Parking: Cars should only be parked in guarded car parks (a necessity due to the rise of break-ins and car theft).

There are only two car parks in the centre, at Plac św. Ducha and Plac Szczepański. Neither is very large and both are very popular. Additional car parks within walking distance of the centre include Plac Kolejowy, by the main railway and bus stations, ul. Biskupia, ul. Zyblikiewicza, ul. Karmelicka, ul. Straszewskiego, and ul. Powiśle by Wawel Castle.

Petrol (gas): Petrol stations are common on major roads; most stay open around the clock and all sell the full range of petrol, diesel and LPG.

V

VISAS AND PASSPORTS

Poland joined the Schengen Block in 2007, meaning that visitors arriving from other Schengen Block countries – regardless of their nationality – are not subject to any border formalities. If arriving from outside Schengen, normal rules apply: you will need a passport to enter the country, and a visa where applicable. Visitors from other European Union countries may enter Poland without a visa and stay for as long as they please, while visitors from the USA, Canada, Australia and New Zealand can similarly enter visa-free, but may only stay for up to 90 days. Almost everybody else will need a Polish or Schengen visa before departing from home. Contact the Polish embassy in your country of residence for more information, well in advance of departure.

Above from far left: traditional way of getting around; Cloth Hall loggia.

Around Main Market Square

Amadeus

Ul. Mikołajska 20; tel: 012 429 60 70; www.hotel-amadeus.pl; €€€

Great Britain's Prince Charles is nothing if not a fine judge of good taste, and that this was his chosen accommodation in Krakow is really all any potential visitor needs to know. Expect sublime service, large rooms full of antique furniture, and fine common areas bursting with genuine Mozart memorabilia. And it all comes at reasonable – if hardly cheap – prices.

Elektor

Ul. Szpitalna 28; tel: 012 423 23 17; www.hotelelektor.com.pl; €€

A Krakow legend, where the draw of the enormous double rooms with separate lounge area has proven to be irresistible for any number of high-rolling visitors. Simply furnished, the rooms are not perhaps as luxurious as they once were, but they offer excellent value for money and the suites especially are almost always reserved months in advance.

Francuski

Ul. Pijarska 13; tel: 012 627 37 77; www.orbis.pl; €€

Though the Francuski is unquestionably a classy place, it is not – as it would like to think – the very best hotel in the city; the rooms are simply too small for such an accolade. Everything else is beyond reproach, however, from the plush bathrooms and exquisite décor to the flawless service and quiet-though-central Old Town location. Good value.

Grand Hotel

Ul. Sławkowska 5–7; tel: 012 421 72 55; www.grand.pl; €€€€

A stone's throw from Main Market Square (Rynek Główny), the Grand is a showcase of neo-Baroque interior design. Every room and suite has been individually crafted, and reception staff are instructed to tailor the needs of the guest to the correct room. All have great bathrooms, Wi-fi internet connections and discreetly positioned televisions. If you can stretch your wallet, go for one of the six sublime suites: the Louis XVIth Fireplace Suite is our favourite.

Grodek

Ul. Na Gródku 4; tel: 012 431 90 30; www.donimirski.com; €€€€

During construction of the Grodek in 2005 an important medieval archaeological site was unearthed next door, and was immediately incorporated into the plans as a museum of archaeology. It is such attention to detail – no request is too big – that sets the Grodek apart; that and the wonderful, award-winning interior design: a modern take on Old Krakow with a cheeky Bohemian twist.

Approximate price categories for a standard double room per night:

€€€€	over 600zł
€€€	425–600zł
€€	250–425zł
€	below 250zł

Pałac Bonerowski

Ul. św. Jana 1; tel: 012 374 13 00; www.palacbonerowski.pl; €€€€

One of the most historic buildings in Krakow, which in the 17th century served as both home and bureaux for King Jan Sobieski, a careful and most satisfying conversion has seen it become the city's best hotel. There are eight rooms and six exquisite suites, and if their size is not immediately impressive, the décor and extras, such as the woven carpets, are. All rooms also have the best views of Main Market Square money can buy, while service is good, and there is an excellent wellness centre in the basement where tired feet and limbs can be massaged back to life.

Pod Różą

Ul. Floriańska 14; tel: 012 424 33 00; www.hotel.com.pl; €€€

Located by the Main Market Square in one of the centre's busiest streets, this historic, plush and antique-filled hotel has some impressive period features, such as the mid-19th-century neoclassical entrance portal: a gem worth checking out even if you are not staying here. Recent renovation has done nothing to diminish the history that exudes from all corners. Not to be missed is the on-site Amarone Italian restaurant, which is one of the city's best. *See also pp.70 and 71.*

Stary

Ul. Szczepańska 5; tel: 012 384 08 08; www.stary.hotel.com.pl; €€€€

In a building that was for more than a century the home of wealthy Krakow industrialists, this gorgeous pile has been renovated into a sublime hotel that combines the old seamlessly with the new. So while the rooms are wooden-floored and retain their character – including original frescoes in some cases – the bathrooms are high-tech, all with Jacuzzi and marble tiling. Some rooms have small balconies with views to Main Market Square.

Wentzl

Rynek Główny 19; tel: 012 430 26 64; www.wentzl.pl; €€€

You want views of Main Market Square? Try the Wentzl – it is *on* Main Market Square. This place may lack the sheer opulence of others, but the rich colours and personal décor make it a home from home. Staff are friendly in a number of languages, and the service – as well as the location, of course – certainly makes up for the rather poky and slightly overpriced rooms.

Wit Stwosz

Ul. Mikołajska 28; tel: 012 429 60 26; www.wit-stwosz.com.pl; €€

A couple of minutes' walk from Main Market Square, this historic building dating from the 16th century has recently been renovated in a traditional style. For what you are paying you really have no right to expect quite so much – the huge, comfortable beds and large windows that swamp the rooms with bags of lights, for example. For families the triples are great value, and they offer possibly the sweetest baby cot ever seen in a hotel in Poland. An atmospheric cellar restaurant serves great Polish food.

Above from far left: neo-Baroque interior at the Grand Hotel; Francuski Hotel staircase.

Hotel Prices
Accommodation will likely be your biggest expense in Krakow. While rooms are most expensive in high season (July and August), Krakow's emergence in recent times as a year-round destination means that hotel prices stay fairly stable throughout the year. A lack of business travellers means that few hotels lower their rates at weekends either. However, there is a wide range of accommodation to choose from: with more than 50 hostels, the budget-seekers have as much choice as the well-to-do.

Around Wawel Hill

Copernicus

Ul. Kanonicza 16; tel: 012 424 34 00; www.hotel.com.pl; €€€€

Hiding behind a wrong-footing Renaissance façade is a small (there are just 29 rooms and suites) modern hotel, with a pool – housed in an old wine cellar – and atrium courtyard, a short walk from Wawel Hill. The rooms may all have Jacuzzis and air conditioning, but all are equally regal in their décor: woodcarvings and marble abound amid rich wallpaper and deep carpets. Service carries a personal touch.

Novotel Krakow Centrum

Ul. Kościuszki 5; tel: 012 299 29 00; www.orbisonline.pl; €€€€

It may be part of a chain, but this gem – located west of the city centre on the banks of the Wisla – is a sound option for its array of extras. The swimming pool is huge, the restaurants excellent and the rooms both comfortable and cosy, even if they are all decked out in corporate colours. From the upper floors there are great views of Wawel, and as they come at no extra cost be sure to ask for one when you reserve or check in.

Qubus Krakow

Ul. Nadwiślańska 6; tel: 012 374 51 00; www.qubushotel.com; €€

If the modern design isn't quite to your taste, then the views from the top-floor swimming pool – yes, you read that right – over the old centre of Krakow certainly will be. Rooms

are all well furnished if a little spartan, and the televisions must be among the biggest in the city. Good service and a reasonable rack rate make this a decent choice for bargain-hunters.

Radisson SAS

Ul. Straszewskiego 17; tel: 012 618 88 88; www.radissonsas.com; €€€

Swedish-owned and -operated luxury, where the rooms – decorated in pastel shades – are large, and the service is as fussy or as discreet as you want it to be. Bathrooms are a particular treat, with their heated floors, wide range of complimentary cosmetics and super-soft robes. There is, of course, an on-site sauna, good restaurants and a lazy, comfortable lobby bar. Surprisingly affordable.

Sheraton Krakow

Ul. Powiśle 7; tel: 012 662 10 00; www.sheraton.com/krakow; €€€€

Well placed on the Wisła Embankment for both the Old Town and Wawel Castle, the Radisson is a Krakow institution. Even those who do not stay in its fine rooms – which pack a big punch in a small space – will often drop by to indulge them-

Approximate price categories for a standard double room per night:

€€€€	over 600zł
€€€	425–600zł
€€	250–425zł
€	below 250zł

Above from far left: a room and a view at the Stary (see p.113).

selves at one of the great restaurants and bars. Indeed, the Someplace Else bar *(see also p.17)*, with its television screen showing sports and its Tex-Mex restaurant, is one of the most popular expatriate hang-outs in the whole of Poland. The swimming pool is a bonus.

Kazimierz

Abel

Ul. Józefa 30; tel: 012 411 87 36; www.hotelabel.pl; €€

In the heart of the Kazimierz district, this historic hotel offers 33 immaculate and brightly coloured if a little basic rooms for a great price. All rooms have en suite facilities, though note that some lack air conditioning, which is not cool in Krakow in high summer. What we love best is the sparkling service from happy smiling staff and the exquisite wooden staircase that leads up to the rooms.

Eden

Ul. Ciemna 15; tel: 012 430 65 65; www.hoteleden.pl; €€

Carefully restored 15th-century building now opened as a hotel in the heart of Kazimierz. It is aimed mainly at Jewish visitors with its kosher restaurant and what we are led to believe is the only *mikvah* (Jewish ritual bath) in the country. There is a sauna, a salt cave (we kid you not) and a delightful garden, too. Good value.

Ester

Ul. Szeroka 20; tel: 012 429 11 88; www.hotel-ester.krakow.pl; €€€

Newish hotel in the heart of Kazimierz, opposite the Old Synagogue museum, and within walking distance of Wawel Castle. Its small scale (only 50 guests fit in when full) lends a personal touch, and staff are friendly. Rooms are fine, decorated in pleasant colours, but it is a little overpriced. A smart, contemporary-style restaurant serves Polish and Jewish cuisine. There's a bar in the cellar and parking spaces.

Klezmer-Hois

Ul. Szeroka 6; tel: 012 11 12 45; www.klezmer.pl; €€

Located on the principal street of the Kazimierz district, near the Tempel and Remuh synagogues, this *fin de siècle* town-house hotel has an attractive café and restaurant. The rooms are large and clean, if a little basic, and they represent decent value for the price.

Around Planty

Andels

Ul. Pawia 3; tel: 012 660 00 00; www.andelscracow.com; €€€€

Following on from the success of a sister establishment in Prague, this modern hotel is as lovely inside as it is ugly from the exterior. Interior design is the main draw here, then, with the powerful reds, Cubist furniture and cutting-edge technology in the rooms (think plasma TV screens and sleek DVD players) suggesting that this place is more a business than tourist choice. Find it opposite the railway station.

Ascot

Ul. Radziwiłłowska 3; tel: 012 384 06 06; www.ascothotel.pl; €€
Equidistant from the station and from Main Market Square, this modern hotel offers pretty standard rooms at a nevertheless decent price. The doubles are a bit small, though the triples and family rooms are very well sized and offer good value. All rooms have good bathrooms, air conditioning and super-fast internet connection. Common areas are a bit dull, but the staff who work here are helpfulness personified. Decent buffet breakfast.

Campanile

Ul. św. Tomasza 34; tel: 012 424 26 00; www.campanile.com.pl; €€
When it comes to Campanile hotels you know exactly what you are going to get: effficient and great service, small but well- equipped and great-value rooms decorated in the company's flagship colours of cream and green, and one of the city's best buffet breakfasts. Rooms on the upper floors have views of Planty.

Europejski

Ul. Lubicz 5; tel: 012 423 25 10; www.he.pl; €
A few minutes' walk from the Planty gardens and Juliusz Słowacki Theatre, this period building offers flexible accommodation, including an attractive 'mansion-block apartment suite' at around the price of a double in a town-centre hotel. Cheaper rooms are also available. There is a stylish bar, a good restaurant and parking.

Fortuna

Ul. Czapskich 5; tel: 012 422 31 43; www.hotel-fortuna.com.pl; €€
This newly renovated period building contains a great little hotel with cosy rooms which may have seen better days, and a nicely furnished restaurant, café and bar, and is located in a neighbourhood of eclectic late 19th-century architecture. Within walking distance of the city centre, it offers free car parking: almost unheard of in Krakow.

Pollera

Ul. Szpitalna 30; tel: 012 422 10 44; www.pollera.com.pl; €€
Beyond the classical façade, this hotel – situated opposite the Juliusz Słowacki Theatre and Holy Cross Church – offers delightful Secessionist interiors, including a superb floral stained-glass window on the staircase. Rooms are well sized and have antique furniture, deep, relaxing beds and original wooden flooring. Some bathrooms have shower only, no bathtub.

Polski Pod Białm Orłem

Ul. Pijarska 17; tel: 012 422 11 44; www.podorlem.com.pl; €€

Approximate price categories for a standard double room per night:

€€€€	over 600zł
€€€	425–600zł
€€	250–425zł
€	below 250zł

Classical building next to the Czartoryski Museum and Florian's Gate, overlooking the original city walls, that incorporates a superb and very comfortable hotel. Though the rooms are a little bare, they are complemented by good bathrooms and the apartments are well worth the extra if you can afford them. Common areas are decorated with fine tapestries and reproductions of classic works of Polish art.

Polonia

Ul. Basztowa 25; tel: 012 422 12 33; www.hotel-polonia.com.pl; €€
Opened in 1917, a thorough refurbishment in 2007 has spruced up this elegant, neoclassical hotel. Situated by a key traffic junction, the thick double glazing ensures a peaceful night's sleep in all of the comfortable – if spartan – rooms. Well located for sightseeing, the hotel is directly opposite the Planty Gardens, and a few minutes from the main railway station. Extras include a beauty parlour and parking.

The Secret Garden Hostel

Ul. Skawińska 7; tel: 012 430 54 45; www.thesecretgarden.pl; €
The Secret Garden is a wonderful hostel that puts to rest the notion that budget accommodation also has to mean, gloomy, dirty and seedy. This colourful place has comfortable dorm rooms as well as simple, immaculately clean private doubles, triples and quad rooms. Add in free Wi-fi, use of a washing machine, lockers and luggage storage, and you have the perfect backpacker stopover. And yes, it has a secret garden.

Grand Hotel Stamary

Ul. Kościuszki 19; tel: 018 202 45 10; www.stamary.pl; €€€€
Luxury has never come cheap in Poland, yet seldom has value for money been so high. For considerable expense you should expect large rooms, decorated in *fin de siècle* style yet all featuring the latest in modern gadgets and conveniences. The service is exemplary from all of the immaculately attired staff. Only the location (next to the resort's grotty bus station) lets it down a little, but once you're inside the hotel, you won't mind.

Mercure Kasprowy Zakopane

Ul. Szymaszkowa; tel: 018 201 40 11; www.mercure.com; €€€
A short walk from the resort centre, this hotel is a fairly standard Mercure affair (meaning good-quality, large and superior three-star rooms decorated in corporate orange), set apart from the bunch by its location at the foot of Gubałówka: most rooms have stunning views.

Villa Marilor

Ul. Kościuszki 18; tel: 018 206 44 11; www.hotelmarilor.pl; €€
Located in a gorgeous 19th-century villa, this hotel makes good use of the huge rooms, with high ceilings and enormous pieces of furniture. Most of the rooms have large balconies, and a few have lovely mountain views: ask for one of these when you make a reservation.

Above from far left: the Pollera's rooms have antique furniture; some hotels' facilities include salt rooms for 'natural healing'; the Pollera's classical façade.

Zakopane
Although its population is only around 30,000, Zakopane receives as many as 2 million visitors per year. This means that if you're planning a visit, you should book your accommodation well in advance, especially during the peak season between Christmas and the beginning of March.

RESTAURANTS

Eating out is one of the pleasures of visiting Krakow. There is a wealth of good restaurants in the city, and almost all have outside seating during the summer. While Polish cooking itself is tasty and filling enough to keep anyone happy for a short trip *(see pp.14–15)*, the cosmopolitan nature of Krakow means that there is also a vast range of restaurants serving a variety of cuisines from all over the world. Even vegetarians – neglected in other parts of Eastern Europe – will have plenty to choose from (although watch out for the ubiquitous pork fat). Waiting staff in all but the lowliest of city-centre restaurants speak English.

Around Main Market Square

Carlito

Ul. Floriańska 28; tel: 012 429 19 12; daily 10am–11pm; €€

Offering perhaps the best views of lively ul. Floriańska, Carlito's is one of those great restaurants that attracts a loyal clientele who come here time after time. Serving great pizza baked on a clay oven amidst a full menu of good trattoria food, expect a loud, boisterous and ebullient time with hundreds of other happy diners.

Prices are for a two-course meal for two with a good bottle of wine:

€€€€	over 170zł
€€€	100–170zł
€€	50–100zł
€	below 50zł

CK Dezerter

Ul. Bracka 6; tel: 012 422 79 31; Sun–Thur 9am–11pm, Fri–Sat 9am–midnight; €€

With dishes from all over Central Europe on offer (recommended is the *bograzsgulas*, a Hungarian stew cooked very slowly in a kettle suspended over an open fire), you are bound to find something here you like. There is a surprisingly good choice for vegetarians, and though the place itself is a little gloomy inside, it is homely and a haunt of both locals and visitors.

Copernicus

Ul. Kanonicza 16 (Copernicus Hotel); tel: 012 424 34 21; daily noon–11pm; €€€€

The menu here offers perhaps the most adventurous Polish food in the land. With outstanding dishes such as venison paté served with marinated forest mushrooms merely appetisers for the mains, like the quail presented on cabbage leaves and roasted potatoes, make sure you arrive hungry. The surroundings are as luxurious as the food, and the cost is as astronomically high as you would expect.

Cyklop

Ul. Mikołajska 16; tel: 012 421 66 03; daily noon–11.30pm; €€€

This is a friendly place whose simple décor follows the familiar trattoria formula. It enjoys a reputation for serving the best pizza in town, which is cooked in a traditional, wood-fired oven. It is

deservedly popular, so expect to queue during peak hours or even share a table: it is all part of the fun; reservations are simply not taken.

Cyrano de Bergerac

Ul. Sławkowska 26; tel: 012 411 72 38; daily noon–11pm; €€€€

A regular and proud winner of the *Best Restaurant in Galicia (Lesser Poland)* award. This achievement might not sound like a big deal in a region not known for the quality of its dining establishments, but Cyrano de Bergerac would be a contender whatever the locale or standard of competition. This is opulent dining in the extreme, with prices to match. The fillet steak is excellent, as are the Polish highlights, such as *pierogi* (small dough parcels filled with anything from minced pork or beef to cabbage and potato or sweet berries). A superb list of French wines befits the superior wine cellar setting of high ceilings and antique furniture. There is also a delightful courtyard garden for alfresco dining in the summer months.

Da Pietro

Rynek Główny 17; tel: 012 422 32 79; daily 12.30–11.45pm; €€€

A spacious and elegant cellar restaurant with professional, attentive staff and an engaging 'smart-casual' atmosphere. It has a deserved reputation for reliable, enjoyable Italian food, comprising all that country's classic dishes, including some of the best pork steaks we have tasted in Poland and a sensational *bistecca fiorentina*. It is no wonder that people keep coming back for more.

Floriańska

Ul. Floriańska 43; tel: 012 421 08 70; daily 1–11pm; €€€

While ul. Floriańska itself is looking increasingly downmarket with its souvenir stalls and snack bars occupying almost every available square inch, this restaurant is attempting to reclaim the street for a more upmarket crowd. Expect fine Italian food, including a sensational goose carpaccio served with rocket and pine nuts.

Gehanowska

Rynek Główny 43; tel: 012 422 93 78 ext.17; daily 8am–midnight; €€€

A classy, august venue with plenty of wood panelling, oil paintings and delicate crockery. Principally aimed at a pensioned and prosperous crowd, Gehanowska is a Krakow institution. Excellent desserts and a small selection of neatly folded world press.

Grand Hotel

Ul. Sławkowska 5–7; tel: 012 421 72 55; www.grand.pl; €€€

In accordance with its name, this is a grand restaurant – classic dishes are served by waiters familiar with old-world standards of courtesy against a background of historic décor. Staff members will help translate a menu that comprises Polish specialities such as sole Walewska, trout and perch dishes, as well as modern European favourites. The dining room is a showcase of elegant Secessionism, with a stained-glass dome and ornate galleries at the mezzanine level.

Above from far left: pizzas at Carlito; salmon at Szara *(see p.120)*; *barscz,* a red beetroot soup; plac Nowy in Kazimierz is a good place to head for bars.

Last Orders
Many of Krakow's restaurants close surprisingly early, and most take their last kitchen orders some time before the published closing time. Arriving at any restaurant much after 10pm will usually warrant shakes of the head and the words 'Kitchen's closed'.

Boiled Cabbage

Don't pass up an opportunity to try *gołąbki*: boiled cabbage leaves stuffed with mince, onion and rice. Legend has it that King Kazimierz IV fed his army *gołąbki* before defeating the Teutonic Knights at Malbork in 1460. Subsequent Polish military failures have often been blamed on a lack of *gołąbki*.

Indus Tandoor

Ul. Sławkowska 13–15; tel: 012 423 22 82; daily noon–10pm; €€€

Photographs of India's finest palaces line the walls of Krakow's finest Indian restaurant. Poles have yet really to take to Indian food, so expect a solely foreign clientele, and dishes which will not be as hot as you would expect. Ask the waiter nicely, however, and he will ask the chef to spice things up for you.

Metropolitan

Ul. Sławkowska 3; tel: 012 421 98 03; Mon–Sat 7.30am–midnight, Sun 7.30am–10pm; €€

Metropolitan is one of the chicest restaurants to have opened in Krakow in recent years. The architectural blend of assorted styles into a 'modern classic' look complements a fine menu that covers a wide range of Italian, French and Polish cuisine. The *barszcz (borscht)* is excellent, and the service is attentive.

Piwnica u Szkota

Ul. Mikołajska 4; tel: 012 422 15 70; daily 12.30–11pm; €€

In keeping with its name – which means 'The Scotsman's Cellar' – the staff are dressed in kilts. The menu does

> Prices are for a two-course meal for two with a good bottle of wine:
>
> | | |
> |---|---|
> | €€€€ | over 170zł |
> | €€€ | 100–170zł |
> | €€ | 50–100zł |
> | € | below 50zł |

feature Scotch egg and haggis, but these are secondary to a wide choice of European and Polish dishes typified by frog's legs in breadcrumbs, *żur* (rye soup) and pork stuffed with prunes.

Pod Osłoną Nieba

Ul. Grodzka 26; tel: 012 422 52 27; Mon–Thur 9am–11pm, Fri–Sun 9am–4am; €

This is an excellent budget option, and good for a change. Cheap kebabs – widely regarded as Krakow's best – are served to a mixed crowd of hungry tourists and late-night, clubbing locals. Order at the counter, then choose to eat in or take away. You can't miss the place; there is a queue outside at all hours of the day.

Szara

Rynek Główny 6 (corner ul. Sienna); tel: 012 421 66 69; daily 11am–11pm; www.szara.pl; €€€€

Understated, discreet, but quite excellent, Szara is now a mainstay of the Main Market Square (Rynek Główny), and an essential part of a trip to Krakow. Don't panic if you can't bag an outside table: inside is a treat, with high ceilings and large tables only adding to the joy of dining here. The food lives up to its surroundings, with delicious dishes such as roe-deer fillet in cranberry and creamy green pepper sauce all rather cutting-edge for Polish cuisine.

Taco Mexicano Cuatro Elementos

Rynek Główny 19; tel: 012 429 52 99; daily noon–11pm, Thur–Sat

Above from far left: a sign for and the inside of Szara; dessert at Floriańska (see p.119); the city has a multitude of cafés.

noon–midnight; www.cuatro elementos.pl; €€€

The stone cellar interior of this taco and tapas bar is a nice enough place to eat, and the food is surprisingly good. This is a spicy and refreshing change from the Polish/European restaurants that otherwise have a monopoly on the Old Town. The nachos are tasty, though the portions are small, and the main courses are better value: try the *Chihuahua burritos*.

U Babci Maliny

Ul. Sławkowska 17; tel: 012 422 76 01; daily 11am–9pm; €

In keeping with its name ('At Your Granny Malina's'), this eatery serves up dishes typically cooked by a Polish granny. It's all great value. Classic peasant food – fermented rye soup with potatoes and sausage, *grochowka z grzankami* (pea soup with croutons), *placki ziemniaczane* (grated potato pancakes) – is served in generous quantities. Order at the counter and pick up a number, which flashes on a small screen when your meal is ready. Collect the food yourself, and take your finished plates to the hatch.

U Pani Stasi

Entrance at Mikołajska 16; tel: 012 421 50 84; daily 12.30–5pm; €

This restaurant presents the cheapest way to enjoy good home cooking. The way to approach it is via a passageway to an inner courtyard, where you will probably have to join the queue. The menu posted by the door and the few that circulate inside are

in Polish only, but don't expect waitresses to listen patiently if you don't speak the language (or even if you do). The restaurant opens at 12.30pm and closes when the food has all been eaten, usually by late afternoon. *Barszcz* (beetroot soup), buckwheat and *pierogi* (ravioli filled with curd cheese and mashed potatoes or, for dessert, apples) are recommended. It's not a place to linger – tell the cashier on the till what you had and pay up.

Wentzl

Rynek Główny 19; tel: 012 429 57 12; daily 1pm–midnight; www.wentzl.pl; €€€€

A Krakow legend. Wentzl offers a classic Polish menu extended by Viennese specialities. Given its imposing pavement façade and the ground-floor café's icing-sugar colour scheme, the 'fine-dining' restaurant in the cellar is something of a surprise, as is the quality of the fresh Hungarian foie gras. The décor is best described as a meeting of vaulted antiquity with postmodern metalwork sculptures.

Zapiecek

Ul. Sławkowska 32, tel: 012 422 75 95; 10am–9pm; €

Local speciality *pierogi* (a kind of Polish ravioli) stuffed with a seemingly endless variety of favourite fillings are served here. Order and pay for what you want from the counter, then move along and pick up your food from the hatch.

Snacks

For snacks, look out for street stalls selling *zapiekanki*, a kind of Polish pizza made of sliced baguette topped with cheese, mushrooms and ketchup. Also popular are *kiełbasa*, rich sausages served with sweet mustard and a slice of bread.

Smoking

Most Krakow restaurants are notoriously smoky: though all should – by law – have a well- separated non-smoking section, this can often be little more than one tiny table in a forgotten corner.

Kazimierz

Anytime Sandwich & Pizza Bar

Ul. Estery 16, tel: 012 432 30 70; 9am–10.30pm; €

Anytime (until 10.30pm at least) is right for good, cheap Italian food in a crowded, bustling atmosphere where the staff go out of their way to be friendly, and shame far more expensive places in the process. There's free Wi-fi, and you can take away if you want.

Arka Noego

Ul. Szeroka 2; tel: 012 429 15 28; daily 10.30am–11pm; €€

All aboard Noah's Ark for all sorts of kosher treats, from Czech wines to Israeli beers. The food is unfussy but comes in huge portions at cheap prices, and the groups of visiting Jews who throng to the place seldom have any complaints. There is live music most evenings, which warrants a compulsory surcharge.

Bagelmama

Ul. Podbrzezie 2; tel: 012 431 19 42; Tue–Sun 10am–9pm; €€

The best thing ever to happen to lunchtime in Krakow. Serving the best bagels in Poland, this place is hardly a restaurant, as you have to eat standing up or take away, but it nevertheless serves great food from its open kitchen. Every kind of bagel (cinnamon, garlic) you can think of can be complemented with just about any topping you can dream up: try curry sauce. Recently expanded its menu to include some Tex-Mex nibbles.

Dawno Temu na Kazimierzu

Ul. Szeroka 1; tel: 012 421 21 17; daily 10am–midnight; €€€

This terrific little restaurant is disguised to look like a row of early 20th-century traders' shops and is topped with awnings relating Kazimierz's Jewish past. Inside it is a riot of antiques – all bought, found or scrounged in the area – with an enjoyable clutter that is hard to dislike. The food is pretty standard Jewish fare, though note that the restaurant is not kosher.

Endzior

Plac Nowy 4b/12; tel: 012 429 37 54; Mon–Sat 10am–midnight; €

Don't be scared off by first appearances. This hole in the wall has all sorts (from lunching schoolboys to smart businessmen) queuing up for its legendary *zapiekanka* (a kind of Polish pizza – essentially a sliced baguette covered with mushrooms and melted cheese and smothered in ketchup) served by miserable, grunting staff through a tiny hatch. A little piece of Krakow, nay Poland, that will hopefully never, ever disappear.

Prices are for a two-course meal for two with a good bottle of wine:

€€€€	over 170zł
€€€	100–170zł
€€	50–100zł
€	below 50zł

Rubinstein

Ul. Szeroka 12 (Rubinstein Hotel);
tel: 012 384 00 07; daily
noon–10pm; €€€€

Found on the ground floor of the
hotel of the same name, the Rubinstein is a sumptuous place where the
waiters are immaculately dressed in
dinner jackets, and guests are
expected to be at least reasonably
smartly attired. There is a good
number of fish dishes on the menu
here – something of a rarity in
Krakow – though such luxuries come
at a high price. The wine list is short
but perfect.

Around Planty

Senacka

Ul. Grodzka 51 (Senacki Hotel); tel:
012 421 11 61; daily noon–11pm;
€€€

Situated in the hotel of the same
name, this restaurant is a red-brick
gem, whose rather ambitious menu
nevertheless delivers real punch. The
golonka (pork knuckle) is always very
good, served with roast potatoes and
thickly cut pickles, while of the many
desserts the chocolate muffins with
cranberry sauce are as sweet as you
could imagine.

Szabla i Szklanka

Ul. Poselska 22; tel: 012 426 54 40;
daily noon–11pm; €€€

A visit is recommended to this snug
Polish–Hungarian restaurant, adjacent
to the Wawel Hotel. The décor is a
modern take on Hungarian style,
dotted with naive touches and splashes

of colour, and the service is know-
ledgeable and pleasant. Start with the
delectable goose and mushroom pie
with plum sauce, followed perhaps by
veal chops with pumpkin seeds, garlic
sauce and mash, and ginger cake with
rose jam and nuts.

Outside the City Centre

Magnifica

Ul. Jugowicka 10c; tel: 012 252
70 10; daily 7am–10.30pm;
€€€€

This restaurant, located in the Far-
mona hotel, is one of the best of those
to open in Krakow in recent times.
Enjoy contemporary European dishes
in hi-tech surroundings (the whole
place is a Wi-fi hotspot, and it's free),
though you will need to book in
advance if you want a table on the bal-
cony during summer.

Villa Decius

Ul. 28 Lipca 17a; tel: 012 425 33
90; daily 1–10pm; www.vd-restau-
racja.pl; €€€€

It's a bit of a trek to reach this eatery
from the centre of town, and it is off
the scale price-wise, but it's certainly
worth the effort and expense to dine
on well-prepared Italian, Polish and
other European dishes within the
palatial Italianate Renaissance Villa
Decius; the restored building is a
feast in itself. Finely attired waiters
make you feel very special as they
whisk away huge silver domes to
reveal beautifully crafted food, such
as the foie gras lightly sautéed in vin-
tage champagne.

**Above from far
left:** antiques
aplenty in Dawno
Temu na Kazi-
mierzu; a basket
of bagels at Bagel-
mama; upmarket
Floriańska *(see
p.119).*

No Thank You
Be careful when
paying in a Krakow
restaurant: saying
'thank you' when
you hand over
money to a waiter
or waitress signifies
that you do not
require any change.

CREDITS

Insight Step by Step Krakow
Written by: Craig Turp and Ian Wisniewski
Edited by: Alex Knights
Series Editor: Clare Peel
Cartography Editors: Zoë Goodwin and
James Macdonald
Picture Manager: Steven Lawrence
Art Editor: Ian Spick
Production: Kenneth Chan
Principal Photographer: Corrie Wingate
Photography by: Apa/Corrie Wingate and
Apa/Gregory Wrona except: Getty 21T,
Mary Evans 20T, Topfoto 83.

Cover: main image: Allan Baxter/Getty; bottom
left: courtesy of Copernicus restaurant; bottom
right: Michal Grychowski/Getty.

Printed by: Insight Print Services (Pte) Ltd,
38 Joo Koon Road, Singapore 628990

DISTRIBUTION

Worldwide
**Apa Publications GmbH & Co. Verlag KG
(Singapore branch)**, 38 Joo Koon Road,
Singapore 628990
Tel: (65) 6865 1600
Fax: (65) 6861 6438

UK and Ireland
GeoCenter International Ltd
Meridian House, Churchill Way West,
Basingstoke, Hampshire, RG21 6YR
Tel: (44) 01256 817 987
Fax: (44) 01256 817 988

United States
Langenscheidt Publishers, Inc.
36–36 33rd Street, 4th Floor,
Long Island City, NY 11106
Tel: (1) 718 784 0055
Fax: (1) 718 784 0640

Australia
Universal Publishers
1 Waterloo Road, Macquarie Park, NSW 2113
Tel: (61) 2 9857 3700
Fax: (61) 2 9888 9074

New Zealand
Hema Maps New Zealand Ltd (HNZ)
Unit D, 24 Ra ORA Drive,
East Tamaki, Auckland
Tel: (64) 9 273 6459
Fax: (64) 9 273 6479

CONTACTING THE EDITORS

We would appreciate it if readers would alert us
to errors or outdated information by writing to
us at insight@apaguide.co.uk or Apa Publications,
PO Box 7910, London SE1 1WE, UK.

www.insightguides.com

INDEX